"No one I know has the ability to stretch the mind and encourage the heart quite like Ken Boa. His presentation in this book will help all of us to write a different page in the diaries of our present by seeing the last page from God's perspective. This book will be high on my recommended reading list for the men I meet with and seek to mentor God-ward."

Mark L. Bailey, president, Dallas Theological Seminary

"Suffering hits us like nothing else in life. We find ourselves crying out *why* or thinking we don't deserve it. We may rail at God and what we feel is the unfairness of life or the absence of God's care, but unless we can reframe our trials in light of a good, loving and holy God, our trials will make us bitter. This book is a tonic for the soul and full of solid biblical insight. Few are as qualified, compassionate or practical as Ken in terms of offering good spiritual counsel. I commend this book for your journey."

Stuart McAllister, regional director of the Americas, Ravi Zacharias International Ministries

"Relevant, thought provoking and creatively expressed in ways that lead us into new avenues of thinking about old and important issues. In *Rewriting Your Broken Story*, Boa reminds us that how we ask and answer life's biggest questions will determine the quality of our day-to-day lives here on earth from a spiritual perspective. *Rewriting Your Broken Story* helps us break through the paradigms that hold us prisoner and prevent us from seeing life the way it really is."

Pat MacMillan, president, Triaxia Partners

"Søren Kierkegaard was right when he said that we have to define life backwards and then live it forwards. It is the arrival that defines the reason for the departure. It is right thinking about life that gives freedom its map. And as Ken Boa observes in this book, 'an eternal perspective will inform us of something more (and better) than what we can see.' Boa has provided a helpful and hopeful map to guide us through life's journey. I know his words will encourage and challenge you."

Ravi Zacharias, author and speaker

"Some books inform. Others inspire. This one does both, but with a goal that few books reach. Ken's words have the potential to transform and to lift readers into the larger and eternal story of God. *Rewriting Your Broken Story* helped me to better see my smaller story as an opportunity to tell God's larger story by how I live."

Larry Crabb, founder and president, NewWay Ministries

"Ken Boa is one of my favorite authors, and this book epitomizes why. It's deep, it's practical, it's theological, it's emotionally stirring, and it helped me see life in a way that God longs for me to see it so I can live it in the way he wants me to live it. Highly recommended!"

Chip Ingram, senior pastor, Venture Christian Church, teaching pastor, Living on the Edge

"Offering captivating illustrations from an incredible array of angles has long been one of Ken Boa's great gifts. This book is a fascinating journey through history, pop culture, biography, philosophy and the arts. But why take that journey? Because ultimately, we all must wrestle with the fundamental questions of life: Who are we? Why are we here? What's gone wrong? How can we be made whole? This book is a journey through those questions, and Ken a most helpful guide."

John Stonestreet, president, The Chuck Colson Center for Christian Worldview

REWRITING YOUR
BROKEN
STORY

THE POWER *of an* ETERNAL
PERSPECTIVE

KENNETH BOA

IVP Books

An imprint of InterVarsity Press
Downers Grove, Illinois

InterVarsity Press
P.O. Box 1400, Downers Grove, IL 60515-1426
ivpress.com
email@ivpress.com

InterVarsity Press® is the book-publishing division of InterVarsity Christian Fellowship/USA®, a movement of students and faculty active on campus at hundreds of universities, colleges and schools of nursing in the United States of America, and a member movement of the International Fellowship of Evangelical Students. For information about local and regional activities, visit intervarsity.org.

All Scripture quotations, unless otherwise indicated, are taken from THE HOLY BIBLE, NEW INTERNATIONAL VERSION®, NIV® Copyright © 1973, 1978, 1984, 2011 by Biblica, Inc.™ Used by permission. All rights reserved worldwide.

Published in association with the literary agency of Wolgemuth & Associates.

While any stories in this book are true, some names and identifying information may have been changed to protect the privacy of individuals.

Cover design: David Fassett
Interior design: Beth McGill
Images: landscape: Todd Korol/Getty Images
　　　　mountain: Cultura RM/Manuel Sulzer/Getty Images

ISBN 978-0-8308-4461-6 (print)
ISBN 978-0-8308-9437-6 (digital)

Printed in the United States of America ♾

Library of Congress Cataloging-in-Publication Data
Names: Boa, Kenneth, author.
Title: Rewriting your broken story : the power of an eternal perspective / Kenneth Boa.
Description: Downers Grove, IL : InterVarsity Press, [2016] | Includes bibliographical references.
Identifiers: LCCN 2016010692 (print) | LCCN 2016011631 (ebook) | ISBN 9780830844616 (pbk. : alk. paper) | ISBN 9780830894376 (digital) | ISBN 9780830894376 (eBook)
Subjects: LCSH: Christian life. | Storytelling—Religious aspects—Christianity. | Suffering—Religious aspects—Christianity. | Future life—Christianity. | Life—Religious aspects—Christianity. | Eternity.
Classification: LCC BV4501.3 .B595 2016 (print) | LCC BV4501.3 (ebook) | DDC 248.8/6—dc23
LC record available at http://lccn.loc.gov/2016010692

| P | 21 | 20 | 19 | 18 | 17 | 16 | 15 | 14 | 13 | 12 | 11 | 10 | 9 | 8 | 7 | 6 | 5 | 4 | 3 | 2 | 1 |
| Y | 33 | 32 | 31 | 30 | 29 | 28 | 27 | 26 | 25 | 24 | 23 | 22 | 21 | 20 | 19 | 18 | 17 | 16 |

I have been shaped and defined over the years by mutual commitments and covenants with others. I treasure the wealth of real friends who pursue together the common goods of truth as a superior, lasting and incorruptible reality that can be enjoyed in its entirety by more than one person at a time. The best kind of friendship is one that is based on the mutual pursuit of the highest goods: truth, goodness, beauty and the source of all these goods—God.

While there are certainly others who have greatly enriched me, this book is dedicated to twelve covenantal friends with whom I have shared this kind of fellowship:

Bick Cardwell	Peter Spanos
Russ Chandler	Len Sykes
Joe Clamon	Al Van Horne
Bill Fagan	Raymond Walker
Errol Kendall	Archie Wanamaker
Edgar Schafer	Carl Woodruff

The Greeks used to say that "between friends, all is common." In the sixteenth century, Erasmus said that the statement still held true because "nothing was ever said by a pagan philosopher that comes closer to the mind of Christ." I see it still true in my own life. The things of the inner life become richer when they are held in common with treasured friends.

Contents

Your Broken Story

—ɯɯ—

Maybe you were fourteen years old when your parents divorced. Up until that time, you didn't have much to worry about, aside from keeping up your grades. Next thing you knew, you were being asked to decide where you wanted to live! Now you're twenty-eight and alone. It's taken you this long to realize that you never quite recovered from the trauma that hit in your first year of high school. You lost the budding faith you had in God, relationships and the goodness of people. You wonder if this is all there is for you and if you will always feel alone.

Or maybe that's not it. Perhaps you enjoyed a good childhood with no trauma, or you overcame the few obstacles you faced. A beautiful family picture hangs over your fireplace mantle, and you have a job that you love. You are busy and productive and "on the right path" to reaching all your goals—but lately you have realized something that is plaguing you. Your responsibilities are increasing, as are your skills, knowledge and salary. But your physical capacities aren't what they once were. Time seems to pass faster than it ever has before, and you realize with clarity and force that many of the hopes and dreams that you've only just recently been able to define are going to go unfulfilled. You stand face-to-face with your mortality. But why? Couldn't you achieve more if you didn't know that your life would one day end? Life is good, but you're beginning to see that something is wrong with the bigger picture.

Maybe you're an addict. You can't stop taking prescription medications or looking at pornography or drinking or yelling at your wife. Maybe you can't keep a job or a spouse. Maybe you aren't welcome in a lot of places anymore, or maybe everyone welcomes you and thinks you're brilliant because no one knows the truth about you. You are trapped in a cycle of addiction that you cannot seem to escape—the same story, over and over. When wisdom brings a moment of clarity, you realize that you are broken.

Maybe you're a mom, and since your children are old enough to think and do things for themselves, you feel like all you ever do is manage their schedules and drive. And clean house. And cook. And drive some more. And make lunches. And check homework. Plunge a toilet and fall into bed exhausted. You can remember dreams you used to have, but you gave them up for this. You love your family, but this is not the story you imagined when you were younger. There are moments when you wonder why *this* is your life. Somehow, you feel a little lost.

Realizations like these can be devastating for people whose expectations are limited to this planet and its offerings, but they are only moments, not the whole story. Everyone has a broken story, and everyone has a choice. When moments like these come, you can embrace your broken story and repair it by setting it in the context of a greater story, one that begins and ends well. Your pain can bring redemption when it forces you to reexamine what you believe. An eternal perspective can change everything, and it can help you to make sense of the story you are living right now.

> For our light and momentary troubles are achieving for us
> an eternal glory that far outweighs them all. So we fix our
> eyes not on what is seen, but on what is unseen, since what
> is seen is temporary, but what is unseen is eternal. (2 Cor-
> inthians 4:17-18)

An *eternal perspective* is one that sees that while life on earth
is important, it's not all there is. This perspective is anchored in
the faith that what the Bible says about eternity is true: God
knew us before we were born, he is with us while we are on earth,
and Jesus has prepared a place for his followers to one day live
with him forever. There are better things for us that we cannot
see yet. The Bible says that God has set eternity in our hearts
(Ecclesiastes 3:11). And C. S. Lewis says, "If I find in myself a
desire which no experience in this world can satisfy, the most
probable explanation is that I was made for another world."[1] An
eternal perspective acknowl-
edges these longings and believes that God gave them to
us as a reminder to set our
hope on him and on things
that will last forever. When we
begin to develop an eternal
perspective, we take on our
new life in Christ and we see

> **Temporal Perspective:**
> This world is all there is.
> There is no life after death.
>
> **Eternal Perspective:**
> Life on earth is important,
> but there is more than this world
> has to offer. We were made
> for eternity.

everything differently. With this new perspective, we can see the
true story about us; it is a far better story than we could have
ever imagined.

Writing Your Verse

There is a riveting scene in the 1989 film *Dead Poets Society*.[2] On the
first day of school, English professor John Keating (played by Robin

Williams) directs his students' attention to an old trophy case in a dramatic attempt to communicate to these adolescents the truth about mortality—a virtually impossible task because most adolescents have no consciousness of mortality. In the case are pictures of graduates from seventy or eighty years before. As he gathers them around the case, Keating asks one of the students to read a poem, Robert Herrick's "To the Virgins, to Make Much of Time":

> Gather ye rosebuds while ye may,
> Old time is still a-flying:
>
> And this same flower that smiles today
> Tomorrow will be dying.

He tells them that Herrick was right: "We are food for worms, lads. Because, believe it or not, each and every one of us in this room is, one day, going to stop breathing, turn cold and die."

He's right in one sense. From a human perspective, we are food for the worms. It's a grim thought, but we must hold in mind that we believe there's something more than this.

Keating goes on. As they all stand looking at the faces in the case, he moves behind them. The camera moves in closer, and he says:

> They're not that different from you, are they? Same haircuts, full of hormones just like you. Invincible, just like you feel. The world is their oyster. They believe they're destined for great things, just like many of you. Their eyes are full of hope, just like you. Did they wait until it was too late to make from their lives even one iota of what they were capable? Because, you see, gentlemen, those boys are now fertilizing daffodils. But if you listen real close, you can hear them whisper their legacy to you. Go on; lean in. Listen, you hear it?

The students don't know what to do. On this, their first day with this teacher, he seems like a total nutcase. But the boys lean in, and Keating whispers in an eerie, rasping voice:

Carpe. . . . Hear it? Carpe. . . . Carpe diem. Seize the day, boys. Make your lives extraordinary.

The following day, he quotes Walt Whitman's "O Me! O Life!":

O me! O life! of the questions of these recurring,
Of the endless trains of the faithless, of cities fill'd with
    the foolish . . .
The question, O me! so sad, recurring—What good amid
    these, O me, O life?

Answer.

That you are here—that life exists and identity,
That the powerful play goes on, and you may contribute
    a verse.

Looking away, Keating asks the students, "What will your verse be?"

This was not a bad way to try to communicate mortality to kids. Keating's desire, inspired by Henry David Thoreau, was that they begin to "suck out all the marrow of life."

The problem with Keating's speech, though, is that it stops short. It's insightful, but it's fundamentally flawed because it's based on a temporal perspective—the proposition that one should gather all the gusto one can get because after death, there will be no more.

While that scene is very moving, it only presents part of the picture. An eternal perspective invites us to come to an experiential awareness of the brevity of life, just as Keating invited his students to do. But followers of Christ don't stop there. They don't see themselves as "food for worms"; instead they understand that this life is incredibly important *in context*. To Christians, eternity does not begin when we die but at the moment we choose to live in Christ, usually right in the middle of our broken experiences. We do not gather rosebuds with the futile attitude that we will be food for worms; instead we embrace the fact that what we do now has ripple effects into eternity, and our time is meant to be invested.

RESPONSIBILITY AND FOCUS

When we are older, the brevity of this earthly sojourn is much easier for us to grasp than it was for Keating's students. But the invitation the world offers us is to disregard what starts to become obvious, and with that invitation come the tools to do it. While our bodies are demonstrating for us that we are clearly not meant to live here forever, the responsibilities and pressures of this world clamor for our attention over seizing the day in any way. They promise the reward of fulfilled dreams and provide ample distraction from the realization that could be leading us into a deeper trust in God's promises. At this point, when we are busier and maybe more productive than ever, we must force our attention toward what lasts. Reminders of our mortality need not shake us. Instead, we can welcome these interruptions as invitations to reassess our focus.

The apostle Paul attempted to interrupt us with his eternal perspective: "Though outwardly we are wasting away, yet inwardly we are being renewed day by day" (2 Corinthians 4:16). This "deepest you" will go on unharmed by the world into the presence of our loving Father. If we anticipate this, it can help to increase our hope and give us a new quality of existence.

So how do we maintain our eternal perspective? In *A Testament of Devotion,* Thomas R. Kelly says that God has ordered our minds in such a way that we're actually capable of thinking on two levels at one time.[3] It requires practice and willfulness. We all suffer from flabby wills, but we can make a conscious choice to be aware of God's presence, meditate on his word and pray without ceasing while we go about our ordinary tasks. The amazing thing about thinking in this way is that the ordinary begins to take on the character of another plane. As our minds dwell on the spiritual, we begin to see God in everything and everyone, whether we're driving down the road, sitting at a restaurant or flinging out the trash.

One simple and practical way to set this "eternal perspective" in motion is to keep Scripture with you, perhaps by writing a verse on a piece of paper and wrapping it around your debit card. Use a verse such as: "For we are God's handiwork, created in Christ Jesus to do good works, which God prepared in advance for us to do" (Ephesians 2:10). Every time you use your card, you will be reminded that your business is not your own. When you are making wealth, it's God's wealth. When you're with people, they are his people, relationships he's given you, people whom you can serve with eternal values at heart. Everything is sacred if you have grasped this principle.

The context in which you view life will determine if these realizations turn you toward crisis or process. A temporal perspective will inevitably lead you to a crisis. If the world is all there is, becoming less able to do things at exactly the time when we are becoming responsible for doing more can become a collision course. But an eternal perspective helps us avoid that collision and realize that *all* of life is a process, divinely ordained to draw us ever closer to God and his purposes. Those limitations that may have seemed like a curse are a gift! Through this divine process, God *weans us from friendship with the world and builds within us a desire for our true home.*

CRISIS OR PROCESS

An old Pennsylvania Dutch adage contends that we grow "too soon old and too late smart." Is it true? If it doesn't come to our attention sooner, by midlife there will be no getting away from the realization that some of the dreams of our youth are disappearing, and along with them the supposition that we'll have all the time in the world to accomplish our goals.

So now a choice is at hand. We can simply listen to the voice that says we are destined for more, or we can act on what it whispers in our ear. We must evaluate our activities and responsibilities in light of the "something more" for which we are destined. We might need to make adjustments to our lives, but once we have taken our hope off the world's promises and put it firmly back on Jesus, we may find that our faith grows and our trust in him increases. These moments of realization, then, are no longer cause to fear; instead, they are cause for joy and permission to rest.

We let eternity inform our present day and live each day in light of the fact that we will one day see Christ. This is an eternal, biblical way of seeing. It runs contrary to the idea that coming into contact with our mortality is a bad thing; instead, it offers hope. Pain and sorrow, disappointments and shattered dreams in this world get contextualized into God's bigger picture when we begin to see that the story is not over at the end of this life.

When we watch a play and all the important characters die in the end, we call it a tragedy. *Hamlet* is a tragedy. If we see a play and it looks like it's all going to go completely awry, but somehow things turn out well at the end, as in *Much Ado About Nothing*, it's called a comedy. It's not always funny, but it has a happy ending. We are in something not far removed from Dante's *The Divine Comedy*; trouble may abound, but paradise is at hand. All things will end well.

And that is what God wants us to see. All of the pain, sorrow, disappointment and brokenness in our lives can be used to draw us to Jesus. These times can actually become, as we look back, moments of grace. They can shatter our autonomy, our independence and our arrogance. They can cause us to walk in dependence on God and in humility. We can learn to help others out of our own weakness instead of out of our own strength, depending on God's strength instead.

Wisdom will help us loosen our grasp on the illusory hope in the promises of this world. Instead we can embrace the hope of the promises of God's Word—the hope of something better. And this will become the radical difference in our lives. "The hope of glory" (Colossians 1:27) will be manifest in our lives. When our story is part of Christ's story, we have no beginning and no end. Our life goes on forever. Because he lives, we will also live; because he rose from the dead, we will rise from the dead. His destiny is now our destiny; his inheritance is our inheritance.

In light of this, God's plan for us is an incredible concept! And we ain't seen nothing yet! "'What no eye has seen, what no ear has heard, and what no human mind has conceived'—the things God has prepared for those who love him" (1 Corinthians 2:9). We just don't have the imagination to begin to fathom all that God has in store for us. But he promises that any pain we go through is to be considered as nothing compared to what he is offering us!

REMEMBERING WHO WE LOVE

Tell me what you love, and I will tell you who you are.

AUTHOR UNKNOWN

This saying was so popular among European writers from the nineteenth century that it's impossible to determine who said it first. Perhaps it's so popular because it's so insightful. We have been in this world so long that we may be unaware when our attachment to it is growing stronger. We are cautioned against loving the world or anything in it, but we frequently forget. "If anyone loves the world, love for the Father is not in them" (1 John 2:15). John tells us what is in the world: "the lust of the flesh, the lust of the eyes, and the pride of life" (1 John 2:16). We are to avoid the allure of these because they cause us to suppose that temporary things are treasures and that we will always have time at the end of our lives for getting right with God. The world's promises mislead us, and its goods are destined to pass away. "But whoever does the will of God lives forever" (1 John 2:17). We are destined to live forever!

The book of James also tells us that "anyone who chooses to be a friend of the world becomes an enemy of God" (James 4:4). These are strong words, but as we become more aware of and more serious about our relationship with our heavenly Father, we take them to heart. As eternal beings, this is the perspective we must maintain: we can only love one or the other, and we are being called to make a choice.

Jesus spoke strongly about what is important: "You are the ones who justify yourselves in the eyes of others, but God knows your hearts. What people value highly is detestable in God's sight" (Luke 16:15). As we become intentional about our relationship with God, we avoid the foolishness that once caused us to disregard these words. If this text from Luke is true, then it should have a huge impact on the way we live our lives. Our goals should begin to be less oriented toward impressing people and more toward pleasing God. This takes maturity and strength of will; it also takes faith to believe that pleasing God is worth the effort. That is why this shift can only come in the context of a growing relationship with the Father as we remember how much he loves us and wants what is best for our lives. The decisions we make will tell whether or not we believe it.

A REAL-LIFE EXAMPLE

Though Payne Stewart was a nominal Christian when he first gained notoriety as a professional golfer, those who watched him play would not have known it, and neither would the players he mocked for attending Bible studies. Stewart was as well known for his egotism and surliness as he was for his signature uniform of knickers and tam-o'-shanter cap.

But something happened as he watched his friend and fellow professional golfer Paul Azinger battle cancer with grace and faith. It shook Stewart, and he began to attend a Bible study at the home of professional baseball player Orel Hershiser. No one can say what the realization was or when it happened, but Stewart began to change. Those close to him noticed first, and soon the public couldn't help but notice. With a new set of priorities, Stewart was playing less, winning more and thanking the Lord—publicly!—for the changes in his life. After his 1999 win at Pebble Beach, the press stood dumbfounded as Stewart responded to their questions about golf with words about Jesus and told them that he was taking the following fall off in order to spend more time with his family. This professional athlete who had become known for his ambition and rudeness began to be recognized for his peace and goodness. Stewart was living a new story.

British golfer Colin Montgomerie played against Stewart and the American team on the last day of the 1999 Ryder Cup. American fans heckled Montgomerie all day, and things were getting tense. Stewart sacrificed his own concentration several times to point out the unruly conduct of his fans to tournament personnel. After Justin Leonard sealed the US victory, Montgomerie and Stewart continued to play out an intense round. But the heckling of Montgomerie became too much. On the final hole, just when it looked like Stewart would emerge victorious, he picked up the ball and handed it to Montgomerie, conceding the match. Even years later, Montgomerie says he will never forget that day or that man.

It turns out that 1999 was not only the height of Stewart's career but also the end of his life. On October 25, Stewart died in a plane crash. But before his death, he had safely placed his story in the center of Christ's story. Stewart's transformation began because his friend Azinger lived a convicted life, showing Stewart that eternity was worth another kind of effort. At Stewart's funeral, Azinger said, "Payne Stewart has finished the race, he has kept the faith, and now the crown of righteousness is his."

When these moments come that bring you to the realization that you are broken, that you are lost or that your story is just not what you hoped it would be, it is a gift. It is wisdom whispering for you to seize the day. Listen closely. Wisdom is not reminding you to simply make the most out of life and gather rosebuds before it's too late. Wisdom is telling you that you are here for a reason, that life exists because of God, and that your identity and story is with your Creator. God's powerful play will go on with or without you, but he has placed you on the stage, in *his* story, and you're invited to contribute a verse.

What will your verse be?

—◊—

In the rest of this book, we will look at how to set the scene for your story in an eternal context, how to find hope when your story hits a snag, how to return to the storyline when you've strayed from it, how to fight temptation, how to leave a permanent mark and how to set your story in motion, leaving a legacy behind.

FOR FURTHER REFLECTION

After reading each chapter, consider taking a day off from reading to practice what you've learned. Each chapter is followed by a section with questions, Scripture to ponder and practices that will bring you closer to the heart of God. If you aren't in the practice of keeping a journal, now might be a good opportunity to start one.

1. If you're reading this book, there's a good chance that you relate to the concept of a "broken story." Write down what is "broken" in your story.

2. Have you ever thought about what it means to set your story in the context of God's greater story? If you're trying to figure out how to get your story back into the context of God's story, reflect on how you got off track.

3. What was the good in what Professor Keating told his young students in *Dead Poets Society*? What was the problem with what he said?

4. Has God ever "interrupted" your life with the realization of your own mortality?

5. How strong is your concept of eternity? What do you do to feed your hope? If it is not strong, consider reaching out to someone who could mentor you in this area.

6. Write what you hope will change in your life as a result of reading this book.

Scripture focus. If you have embedded your story in the context of God's great story, there are truths about yourself that will be revealed, great things you may have never known. Read 2 Corinthians 4:16. Consider committing it to memory.

Practice. Consider reading Thomas R. Kelly's book *A Testament of Devotion* (mentioned in this chapter) and putting some of the very tangible and helpful suggestions from that book into practice.

Investing in Eternity

We fix our eyes not on what is seen,
but on what is unseen, since what is seen is
temporary, but what is unseen is eternal.

2 CORINTHIANS 4:18

PARADIGM

Paradigm is a word that has existed for centuries, but it was popularized by Thomas S. Kuhn in his 1962 book *The Structure of Scientific Revolutions*. Since then, it has become part of our vernacular, signifying a set of rules (implicit or explicit) that molds a person's perspective and affects the way one forms a view of the world.

All Christians must make a fundamental paradigm choice: the decision between what is and what seems to be, what will last and what won't—between the *eternal* and the *temporal*. This choice is examined repeatedly in Scripture. Jesus spoke more about the temporal versus the eternal than any other topic. The choice we make is between that which God says will endure and that which won't. Followers of Jesus will naturally want to be a people who treasure what God says is a lasting treasure.

Folk rock band The Byrds popularized a song written by Pete Seeger called *Turn! Turn! Turn!* It was a huge hit based on Ecclesiastes 3. Many of us know the Scripture from the song: a time to weep, a time to laugh, a time to mourn, a time to dance, a time to love, a time to hate, a time for war, a time for peace. In that same chapter, Solomon says, "I have seen the burden God has laid on the human race" (Ecclesiastes 3:10). And here is the key verse: "He has made everything beautiful in its time. He has also set eternity in the human heart; yet no one can fathom what God has done from beginning to end" (Ecclesiastes 3:11). We don't get to see the whole picture now, but one day we will (1 Corinthians 13:12)!

To value what God values, we have to shift from allowing other people and the world around us to shape how we see things to allowing what the Bible says to shape our view of life. We are constantly under pressure to cave in to viewing things like everyone around us does. The world is so ambient, so present and so constant, inviting us to see things from this present darkness rather than from God's perspective. But God has set eternity in every person's heart, and he can use our times of brokenness to rewrite our stories. *Embracing a biblical (eternal) perspective, we move toward the wisdom that will help us understand our present, fleeting opportunities in the context of a very real eternity.*

> **Temporal Perspective:**
> that which relates to this passing world order and will not go on into eternity.
>
> **Eternal Perspective:**
> that which can be sent ahead from this life into the next life and will endure forever. The Bible is written from an eternal perspective, so a biblical perspective or a biblical worldview is also an eternal one.

THE IMPENDING END OF YOUR LIFE

Let's examine this practically. Suppose you go in for a routine physical examination and you're told by your doctor that you have an illness that is not palpable or evident to you but that will be terminal. You've got about a year (or maybe less) to live. You go to two other physicians, and they confirm the diagnosis. There won't be any really obvious effects until the disease reaches its final stages, but you will surely die within a year.

Now, ask yourself these questions:

1. How would this diagnosis affect your vision of life?

2. How would it affect your view of your roles on earth? (friend, parent, daughter, son)

3. How would it affect the way you invest your money and time?

Clearly, such a realization that we have so little time could have a huge impact on us. But understand this: *the degree to which it would alter your present perspective and practice is the degree to which your current view of life and the biblical view of life diverge.* The distance between your current view of life and the biblical view of life is the degree to which you would expect this announcement to have changed your whole perspective and practice in the world. Your vision of life ought to be the same, whether you have one day or thirty years to live.

Second, how would it change your view of your roles? *Are you living in such a way that you regard relationships and treat people as if this could be the last time you'll ever see them?*

And third, how are you investing your money and time? If there has to be a radical modification, you should probably ask yourself why. If you are already spending your money and time for God's purposes, you shouldn't need much adjustment.

Frankly, none of us know that we have even a year. We can't presume on the future. We can't control one day. And so we ought to treasure the opportunities of the present by enhancing the roles we play by serving other people and investing our money and time wisely and well, viewing our service to the people in our lives as service to Christ himself. Only two things will last forever: God's Word and people. We would be wise to invest one into the other, making sure that the remaining days of our stay on this planet have optimal impact and lasting consequences on the lives of other people, leveraging the wealth of this world for eternal gain. That is living from an eternal perspective; that is investing in our eternal future.

Death from a Temporal View: Denial

The temporal perspective usually denies the imminence of death, allowing—almost encouraging—us to believe that we might live forever. We don't want to think about or deal with the idea of death. Doing so would launch an assault against our own perspective and acknowledge our lack of control and the brevity of our lives. Many people are only confronted with the reality of their mortality when they're at a funeral. A funeral is a window of reality, a time of vulnerability. It causes us to question the dash between the birth and death dates on our tombstones.

It's rather striking that, until we're at an event such as a funeral, we fail to see what's right in front of us. We have incredible mechanisms in place that help us avoid what is critical. We dress up cadavers and make them comfy. We put them in cushioned little beds, as if it's going to matter whether they have silk lining or a pillow, and then we refuse to talk about death. We use words like "the departed" and "passed away," euphemisms that help us avoid the healthy reminder a funeral could actually be—to value our lives and remember they won't last forever.

In Ecclesiastes 7:2, Solomon says, "It is better to go to a house of mourning than to go to a house of feasting, for death is the destiny of everyone; the living should take this to heart." He's right; we have to be realistic. We are a strange people who seek to avoid what is obvious. People die around us all the time, yet we continue to act as if death is something that will happen to someone else.

DEATH FROM MY PERSPECTIVE

I don't have the luxury of thinking death is for someone else. For reasons I cannot explain, I have stared death in the face on numerous occasions. It's happened in a variety of contexts; many times it was so serious that I was absolutely sure I was living my last minutes. For example, in the summer of 1978, I went on a three-week Holy Land tour with a friend and fellow graduate from Dallas Theological Seminary Arnold Fruchtenbaum. For part of our tour, we stayed on a kibbutz campsite on the southern shore of the Sea of Galilee. One day, when we had some free time, I thought I would go for a swim alone on the sea. I saw a raft only about a tenth of a mile away from shore and decided to swim out to it and lounge a bit. But that's not how my afternoon went.

The Sea of Galilee is a basin at the bottom of Galilee hill country on one side and the Golan Heights on the other. It is known for being calm and peaceful; the Jews say it's God's favorite of all the seas. However, when winds become trapped in the basin of relatively shallow water, they can cause deadly storms that seem to come out of nowhere. Waves on the small sea have been recorded up to ten feet. If you've heard the story of Jesus calming the storm that terrified his disciples in Matthew 8, this is the same sea.

But it was a beautiful afternoon, and I suppose I wasn't thinking about Matthew 8. I swam out to the raft and then turned around and headed toward shore. On my way back, a storm came out of nowhere. The winds began to move the sea, and like water on a shaking saucer, it was instantaneously tumultuous. I found myself embroiled in the violent movements of the water and couldn't make any progress back to shore. It was difficult just to stay afloat. I kept trying to make progress in the right direction, but the wind and the waves kept pushing me back, and I was far from safety.

This lasted for what seemed to be a really long time, and my energy was spent. I became aware that I wasn't going to make it. I knew I was on the verge of drowning, and my life flashed before my eyes, like in a movie. Time seemed to dilate. I saw so many things in a flash, but I had no experience of terror because I became aware of something bigger than the storm. It was suddenly clear to me that I had a lot of unfinished business on earth. During this profound divine/human dialogue, God told me that my work for him on earth was not complete.

And then I was at the shore. I have no idea how I got there. There was no way I had the strength to swim that distance against those waves. I was just at the edge of the water. But there were rocks on the shore, and they were extremely slippery. I was unable to get a purchase on the rocks so that I could get out of the water. And then it happened again. Suddenly I found myself laid out on a grassy area above the rocks. I have no idea how I got above the rocks. I couldn't have pulled myself out of the water, and there was no one around who could've helped me.

I lay there for a while, caught my breath and reflected on the situation. I knew I had unfinished business, and it was not my time. The message was unmistakable.

It's funny to think now that if I had drowned in the Sea of Galilee, people might have said, "Oh, what a man of God—he died on the sea where Jesus walked." But that was not my fate that day, nor was it my fate on the many other occasions when I came face to face with death.

The flashbacks and that sure sense of "I'm not ready yet; something still has to be done" occurred each time I faced death. And somehow, each time, God pulled me out of there. Disease, an accident, another near-drowning—somehow, he's always given me more time. So now I realize that I'm on borrowed time. Frankly, we all are. Every breath we draw, every beat of our hearts is something given by God. We don't control our time on this planet.

DEATH FROM AN ETERNAL VIEW: NUMBERING OUR DAYS

The sixth and seventh stanzas of Isaac Watts's hymn "O God, Our Help in Ages Past," based on Psalm 90, say:

> The busy tribes of flesh and blood,
> with all their lives and cares,
> Are carried downwards by the flood
> and lost in following years.

> Time, like an ever-rolling stream,
> bears all its sons away;
> they fly, forgotten, as a dream
> dies at the opening day.

At first that sounds really depressing, but what Isaac Watts is really meditating on is Moses' observation of the radical difference between God's eternity and the brevity of our stay on earth. The psalm begins:

> Lord, you have been our dwelling place
>   throughout all generations.
> Before the mountains were born
>   or you brought forth the whole world,
>   from everlasting to everlasting you are God.

You turn people back to dust,
    saying, "Return to dust, you mortals."
A thousand years in your sight
    are like a day that has just gone by,
    or like a watch in the night.
Yet you sweep people away in the sleep of death—
    they are like the new grass of the morning:
In the morning it springs up new,
    but by evening it is dry and withered. (Psalm 90:1-6)

Verse 12 is the key to this Psalm and tells us what we should do if we are to be wise: "Teach us to number our days, that we may gain a heart of wisdom" (Psalm 90:12).

A Hebrew professor I had took this to heart. He combined this verse with verse 10: "Our days may come to seventy years, or eighty, if our strength endures" (Psalm 90:10). So my professor calculated how many days he had left and wrote that number minus one more each day on his calendar. You might think that sounds morbid, but that's what the ancients called a *memento mori*, a reminder of your death. It's like an Ash Wednesday service, when they give you the sign of the cross on your forehead with the ashes. They say, "Remember that dust thou art and unto dust thou shalt return." This is to remind us to use our time wisely because our time on this earth is brief. These things aren't meant to make you morbid. They're meant to remind you to value the days you are given and use them to become wiser.

In Psalm 39:4-7, David, the king after God's own heart, prays:

Show me, LORD, my life's end
    and the number of my days;
    let me know how fleeting my life is.
You have made my days a mere handbreadth;

the span of my years is as nothing before you.
Everyone is but a breath,
 even those who seem secure.

Surely everyone goes around like a mere phantom;
 in vain they rush about, heaping up wealth
 without knowing whose it will finally be.

But now, Lord, what do I look for?
 My hope is in you. (Psalm 39:4-7)

This text is three thousand years old, but the wisdom hasn't changed much. We don't know why we're driven to amass wealth. And we forget or don't ever know what life is about. Isaiah 40:6-8 uses a metaphor similar to the one we saw in Psalm 90, again developing a radical contrast between the temporal and the eternal:

All people are like grass,
 and all their faithfulness is like the flowers of the field.
The grass withers and the flowers fall,
 because the breath of the LORD blows on them.
 Surely the people are grass.
The grass withers and the flowers fall,
 but the word of our God endures forever. (Isaiah 40:6-8;
 emphasis added)

And James contributes this sobering thought: "Why, you do not even know what will happen tomorrow. What is your life? You are a mist that appears for a little while and then vanishes" (James 4:14).

Why do you suppose there are so many texts that invite us to recognize our mortality? Maybe it's because we are so quick to deny or rationalize it away. We long for eternal life, but it's difficult for us. And frequently we're "mistaking Paradise for that home across the road," as Bob Dylan sang in "The Ballad of Frankie Lee and Judas Priest." Though God has wired us with a longing for eternity, we often foolishly behave as if the eternal realm is here and that life here and now on earth is all there is.

People seem more apt to hope for eternity when life is very tough. But many of us living on earth now are among the most affluent and comfortable people who have ever lived here. We have more pleasures than kings once knew. We control our climate with a thermostat. We can go wherever we choose by various modes of transportation. We can command all the great orchestras of the world to play whatever we want at any given moment on phones that fit in our pockets!

These blessings can bring with them an unfortunate consequence: life in the temporal here and now can feel so comfortable that we really can come to prefer it over any hope of a promised, eternal home. And this is a terrible mistake—because if we do that, we live an illusion instead of the truth. This is why moments of brokenness are a gift. They rescue us from complacency and build our longing for what is better.

Pessimistic and Morbid or Hopefully Realistic?

The frequent biblical references to our mortality are reminders. They're not morbid; they point to the most realistic and hopeful approach a person can take. Anyone who has read the grittier stories in the Bible knows that it's realistic. But what is hopeful about this?

The older I get, the faster the years seem to whiz by, and now I can see all the decades of my life almost simultaneously. It's rather odd. I can recollect memories from when I was ten years old as easily as those from when I was thirty years old. And the memories I have from last month are no more vivid than the memories I have of something that happened thirty years ago. I can still see myself at the age of nineteen at the Phi Kappa Alpha fraternity house talking with a couple of my buddies and saying, "Hey guys, we're at the prime, but it'll all be downhill from here." We actually made a covenant. We said, "Let's remember this moment . . . thirty years from now." And darned if I don't remember it. I can see where we were standing by the stairs and then coming to the realization, even at nineteen, of how fleeting life would be. My memory of it is so clear that it could have happened yesterday.

Maybe this is a hint of how God sees things. I look back on my life, and I can see my life almost as a seamless whole because it's an identity that's been shaped by experience. We each have a self that is a continuity of the experiences it takes on. The odd thing is that we can look at time not as a series of events but as a complete unified whole. For God, there is no passing of time. He sees all things in the present tense. We come to see in this way a little bit as we accumulate our own experiences and as the years go by. Perhaps our own minds take on a little more of the eternal when we see this way.

When looking back, we have a clearer picture of the truth. It's always better to know things as they are than to believe things as they seem. It doesn't require divine revelation to realize that everyone dies. The only people who Scripture mentions as never having died at all were Enoch and Elijah, and we shouldn't count on joining in their fate.

But here is where the hope lies: an eternal perspective will inform us of something more (and better) than what we can see. A biblical perspective assures us that the longings we often feel for more than this world can offer are real. They come from something God has placed inside of us. The biblical vision of God's invitation to us is not just forgiveness. That forgiveness means something—that Christ's life can be in us *now*; the new life and our future in him have already begun!

"Now this is eternal life: that they know you, the only true God, and Jesus Christ, whom you have sent" (John 17:3). Eternal life is not just endless life; it is a *new quality of life* that is ours now and will never fade or perish.

Past/Present/Future—Where We Choose to Live

Sigmund Freud would say that all we've got is our past—that we are mechanisms that are defined by our nature and our nurture, and we are very brief. Freud's naturalistic philosophy is extremely discouraging, but it has heavily influenced our culture. A biblical perspective turns this kind of thinking on its head.

You are not defined by your broken past if you are a follower of Jesus. Instead, you are defined by your unbounded future. All the past you'll have on this earth will be a few decades. On the other hand, the future is limitless, an infinite and continual changing process, in which we have new insights and new relationships. We have a glorious destiny, and that gives us a much better context for our present tense.

We must avoid this mistake of living for future prospects, assuming we will have time for doing what we want in our retirement. We have to take all that we can out of each day and relish it, investing it in people who are destined for eternity. What would it be like if we looked at each person in front of us as if we would never see them again, as if this were the most important moment on earth? What if, during our lunch meetings with someone, instead of letting our minds wander to what we have to accomplish when we get back to the office, we esteemed the person we were with as the most important person in the world? What if we focused on that moment? The truth is, at least right now, that's all we've really got anyway.

The biblical vision of God's invitation to you is not only forgiveness but also newness of life and a transcendent hope, a hope that tells you that your longing for eternity is prompted by something real. You have been hardwired by God with eternity in your heart, and you cannot eradicate that longing, no matter how hard you try. You have something in yourself that will not be satisfied by this present world. Admit it, and then you may realize that God is using this time to prepare you for your eternal story in heaven.

FOR FURTHER REFLECTION

1. What influences your perspective? Do you see how culture has influenced you? Make a plan for modifying your paradigm toward an eternal perspective.

2. Go through the exercise from the chapter in which you were asked to imagine going in for a routine physical examination and discovering that you have only one year to live. Answer the following questions:

   • How would it affect your vision of life?

   • How would it affect your view of your roles on earth? (friend, parent, daughter, son)

   • How would it affect the way you invest your money and time?

   Talk about this with someone.

3. In what ways are you "leveraging the wealth of this world for eternal gain"? Or in what ways could you be doing so?

Scripture focus. Part of embedding your story in God's greater story is planning according to your new reality. Consider memorizing Psalm 90:12 or keeping it somewhere visible so you'll be reminded of it.

Practice. God has wired us with a longing for eternity in our hearts. Why not feed that longing? Consider purchasing a book about heaven or spend time studying Revelation 21. Search your Bible with a concordance for passages about heaven throughout the Bible. Don't know which book to read? Try *Sense & Nonsense About Heaven & Hell* by Kenneth Boa and Robert M. Bowman Jr. or Peter Kreeft's *Heaven, the Heart's Deepest Longing.*

The Reversible Paradigm

—ɯ—

E very day, the world implores us to accept its story about us, to chase its promises and believe that it holds our future. But eternity in our hearts reminds us regularly that there is more to this life than we can see. So one day our eyes open; our paradigm shifts, and we make a faith choice. We choose eternal life and eternal hope. But is that it? Once we choose the eternal over the temporal, why do this worldview and hope so easily and frequently escape us? If we've set our story in God's eternal context, why is it so difficult to see ourselves there?

AN IRREVERSIBLE PARADIGM SHIFT

The most celebrated example of a paradigm shift is the Copernican revolution in astronomy. Until the time of Nicolaus Copernicus, the reigning paradigm was Ptolemy's centuries-old geocentric (Earth-centered) system. In his book *Almagest*, Ptolemy mathematically documented his argument that our non-rotating Earth was the center of a terrestrial system, with all other planets orbiting around it. Theologians supposed that if man was the pinnacle of God's creative work, then it made sense for Earth to be the center of everything. Based upon this fallacious understanding of Scripture, the church adopted and advocated Ptolemy's geocentric model. And while there was no warrant for this theology, they held to it (and to Ptolemy's system) dogmatically.

For centuries after, astronomers made many observations that simply didn't fit that model. But when a new system didn't work with the old model, instead of revising their way of seeing, they adopted very clever systems to account for what made no sense. The result was a well-documented, elaborate mathematical system that never completely worked. This old paradigm reigned because most astronomers couldn't accept another.

In 1543, the year of his death, Copernicus published his *De Revolutionibus Orbium Coelestium* (*On the Revolutions of the Celestial Orbs*) presenting his heliocentric (sun-centered) system. Knowing that this hypothesis would meet with a good deal of hostility from the religious establishment and his colleagues, Copernicus waited to publish his book until long after it was written. In it, Copernicus provided a simple and elegant explanation of the movement of the planets and definitively settled the question of the planetary order. In the years that followed, the findings of Galileo Galilei, Johannes Kepler and Isaac Newton provided further support for Copernicus's ideas. By the end of the next century, information supporting the heliocentric model provided a foundation so strong that science would never be able to shift back to the geocentric paradigm.

A REVERSIBLE PARADIGM SHIFT

The Copernican revolution didn't happen in an instant (not even in Copernicus's lifetime), but some paradigm shifts do. Take a look at figures 1 and 2.[1] Whether you see an old woman or young woman in the first image and a duck or a rabbit in the second, depends on your perspective—your paradigm. But that paradigm can change when you learn that the chin line of the young woman is the nose of the old woman or when you find out the rabbit looks right and the duck looks left.

Figures 1 and 2. Do you see an old or young woman? A duck or a rabbit?

Psychologist Joseph Jastrow used the duck-rabbit figure to demonstrate that perception doesn't just depend on the object being perceived. Several other factors must also be considered, including circumstances and mental activity.[2] For example, one study found that, "interestingly, children tested on Easter were more likely to see the figure as a rabbit, whereas when tested on a Sunday in October, they tended to see it as a duck."[3]

We've all seen optical illusions before. We look at the illusion from one point of view and are unable to see it. But after it's pointed out, suddenly we make out what we hadn't seen before and we can see it both ways—reversible visual paradigms.

CHRISTIANITY—A REVERSIBLE PARADIGM

Paradigms can be reversed. While we might hope that "catching" the message of the gospel of Jesus Christ will create a Copernican shift in our lives (and often it feels as if it has), we can become disappointed, as growing Christians, when we find that it has not. *Embracing the eternal view does not ensure our hanging on to it.* Instead, this perspective that we so need slips from our grasp because it's so easy for us to return to the orientation that we have lived in so long before.

COMING TO FAITH—THE ULTIMATE PARADIGM SHIFT

A paradigm shift doesn't generally happen on its own. Our paradigm will only shift when, faced with an undeniable reality, we see something with new eyes.

Coming to faith in Christ is that kind of a thing for many people. Very few people actually grasp what Jesus has accomplished the first time they hear about it. They must hear the message again and again. It's common to find people who may not know or understand the difference between knowing about Jesus and trusting in him, between giving intellectual assent to the truth of Jesus and having a real relationship with him. Sure they can recite the creeds, but they don't understand what it means to know him and be known by him.

But suppose I teach through the Gospel of John or the book of Romans. Eventually, a light may go on, all of a sudden. It might take several teachings, but suddenly a coherent way of seeing emerges, and some students see that this is what it really means to be a follower of Jesus. It's not about just believing in a proposition; it's trusting in a person. There is a huge difference because Christianity is not a religion, it's a relationship. And while the Bible is filled with important propositional truth, the revelation in the Bible was not given to inform us but to transform us. And that revelation demands a response. The message of the gospel is a series of propositions that invite a personal response—a cognitive response, a volitional response and sometimes an emotional response. That response is the paradigm shift that leads to real Christian conversion. (If you'd like to see all this played out in real life, skip ahead for a minute and read the epilogue about Chuck Colson.)

The following is an old story, but it illustrates well the difference between belief and trust in Christ. In 1859, French tightrope walker Charles Blondin traveled across the ocean and came to the Niagara Falls. There he hoped to accomplish something that had never been done. He strung a one-thousand-foot cable across the falls from the Canadian side to the United States side and prepared to walk across.

A large crowd watched as Blondin successfully crossed. Over the course of the next year, he made several more trips across the falls, thrilling the crowd each time with more dangerous stunts. He balanced a chair on the rope and stood in it. He took pictures of the crowd while balancing on the rope. He actually cooked a meal on a small portable cooker and lowered it to an amazed crowd on a ship below. Eventually, he got a wheelbarrow and put a weight in it and rolled it across, which impressed the crowd even more. Then Blondin turned to the crowd and asked, "How many of you believe I could take one of you and put you in this wheelbarrow and roll you across?" Everybody said, "We believe!" But when he asked for volunteers, no one would accept his offer. Tens of thousands believed, but not one trusted. *Belief and trust are two completely different things.*

It occurred to me, though, that there's something wrong with this illustration. Why would anyone get in the wheelbarrow? Why would anyone do such a dopey thing? There would have to be a compelling reason.

So try this: imagine that there was a thick forest behind the spectators and that suddenly the forest caught fire. There was no way of escape. Now things get interesting, and suddenly all the rules change. Now there are only four options for the crowd:

- Option number one: "I'm not here, and it's not hot." Deny your situation until you're burned to a crisp.

- Option number two: take your chances by plunging into the raging water below.

- Option number three: try to go across the tightrope yourself.

- Option number four: get in the wheelbarrow!

Suddenly, the offer to get in Blondin's wheelbarrow looks very attractive. Furthermore, it's not a leap in the dark; it's a step into the light and perhaps your only real hope. He's already demonstrated that he could go to the other side and come back.

And so has Jesus. His crucifixion and resurrection was his going to the other side and coming back, his demonstrable evidence that he is who he claims to be. Entrusting my life to him, sitting in his wheelbarrow (so to speak) is really a reasonable thing to do. My paradigm has shifted, and I can see that choosing not to get into that wheelbarrow is a bad choice, as would be ignoring or rejecting Jesus. With Jesus, there are really only two options because ignoring him is just covert rejection. At the end of the day, you either trust him or you don't.

In Luke 23 we learn of two criminals crucified on either side of Jesus at the cross, and they illustrate this point. They were both mocking him. They were both going along with the crowd, saying, "Come on down from the cross." But then one of them came to a realization. "Wait a minute, now. We suffer justly for our cross, but this man has done no wrong." And then he turned to Jesus: "Remember me when you come into your kingdom." What was Jesus' response? "Truly I tell you, today you will be with me in paradise" (vv. 42-43). Wow!

For a while, we may be comfortable with the cognitive dissonance between what we believe and the evidence. But there finally reaches a point where we can no longer hang onto the old paradigm, and we place our trust in Christ.

MID-COURSE ADJUSTMENTS

A man named Mike worked from home two days a week and found he was very productive there. But lately, he noticed he wasn't so productive anymore. He traced it back to the day he'd brought a small flat-screen TV in from the other room to watch a new show that was going to be talking about his company. He watched the program, turned off the TV and went back to work, but he never moved the television back to the other room. A few days later, an NCAA basketball championship game was on. He turned on the TV for one game and worked while he watched. Over time, he developed a habit of watching TV that distracted him. If Mike was going to get back his productivity, he was going to have to break that habit.

We suffer from a similar problem: after we have placed our trust in Christ, we set aside time to develop an eternal perspective by spending time in prayer and in God's Word. The Spirit's wisdom begins to change us. But before long, we allow distractions to move us away from these practices. First it's something small, and then it's something else. Eventually, we might find ourselves with memories of time we've spent with God instead of present-day experience. That's why it's so important to commit to continually renewing our minds, allowing the Spirit to wash us with the water of the Word by immersing ourselves in Scripture and allowing it to purify us (see Ephesians 5:26 or Romans 12:2).

When you shift to an eternal paradigm, you're in a place of conscious awareness of what your perspective is. You suddenly realize that neutrality is a myth, an illusion. You make a huge adjustment, right in the middle of your life story. You choose God's promises about your life and your future—and with your new eternal story, you set out to live your life in a whole new way.

But after months, or maybe years, something happens. You're still going to church. You haven't renounced your faith or even expressed your doubt, but you're not able to see from an eternal point of view as clearly as you did at first. You're distracted.

Christians repeatedly forget about the price that's been paid for them. They forget what's been done for them and the resources that are now available to them, and though they are still believers, they live as practical atheists. They might not acknowledge this, but it's how they live. We're not talking about a Copernican shift anymore. We're talking about a duck and rabbit situation. Now you see it, now you don't.

For a season, we saw everything from an eternal perspective. But then suddenly we slipped back because it's more comfortable where we came from—we lived in it so long before—and the tide of the world pulled us back to it. This is why there is still spiritual warfare. The Christian life would be so much easier if we could just buy the message of Christ and be instantaneously transported by chariot to heaven. Wouldn't that be easier? But then we would never grow.

It's obvious in the Gospels that Jesus knew his followers would struggle to hang on to their faith in him. And one word he used several times gives us a clue to the fact that he knew we would struggle too. The word? "Daily." He says, "Whoever wants to be my disciple must deny themselves and take up their cross *daily* and follow me" (Luke 9:23, emphasis added). And again, his prayer in Matthew is "Give us today our *daily* bread" (Matthew 6:11, emphasis added). The Christian life can only be lived one day at a time. We come to faith and grow a little at a time. You are *being* "transformed by the renewing of your mind" (Romans 12:2), but you aren't finished. The writer of Hebrews asks you to "encourage one another *daily* . . . so that none of you may be hardened by sin's deceitfulness" (Hebrews 3:13, emphasis added).

The choice must be made again and again: temporal or eternal? We must *choose each day* whether we will live as if this world is all there is or as if our earthly existence is a brief pilgrimage during which we learn and grow and are prepared for eternity. How quickly we forget the brevity of life and deceive ourselves into thinking that we have all the time in the world. We forget the reality that people around us are dying all the time.

Those of us who have lived through more than a few decades know this experience: you get to a party with old friends who haven't seen you in ten or fifteen or maybe even thirty years, and the first thing they say is "My, you look marvelous!" But let's be frank: we don't look marvelous; we look terrible when compared with how we looked when we were younger.

If we base our hope on the notion that this world is all there is, we're eventually going to have to deny the reality of what time is doing to our bodies. We're *not* going to live forever. And believing that we are doesn't provide any meaning, purpose or hope. It especially doesn't help when you get home from that party and look in the mirror.

RESTING IN GOD'S PROMISES

Now faith is confidence in what we
hope for and assurance about what we do not see.
This is what the ancients were commended for.

HEBREWS 11:1-2

If you haven't read Hebrews 11, you should go do it. It's a reality check. The men and women in Hebrews 11 embraced the perspective of the eternal being more valuable than the temporal. Many of them never saw the fulfillment of the promises that God

had made to them. They trusted that the eternal would come
and bring the fulfillment of their hopes.

> All these people were still living by faith when they died.
> They did not receive the things promised; they only saw
> them and welcomed them from a distance, admitting that
> they were foreigners and strangers on earth. . . . Instead,
> they were longing for a better country—a heavenly one.
> Therefore God is not ashamed to be called their God, for
> he has prepared a city for them. (Hebrews 11:13, 16)

Among these heroes of faith was Abraham. The chapter says he
was "looking forward to the city with foundations, whose architect and builder is God" (Hebrews 11:10). He wasn't at home
here. And neither will you ever truly be home in this world.
These faith heroes were ordinary people who trusted in God and
became great. Though they didn't receive God's promises in this
life, they died in faith, clinging to the hope that God had something more in store for them.

Their perspective was eternal. They made a commitment: "I'm
never going to embrace this world's temporal promises, which
cannot be counted on. My hope must be in the eternal promises
of God because only God can truly promise what will last and
stay with me to my true home in eternity."

Those who have embraced a temporal paradigm treat what is
temporary as though it were eternal and the eternal as though it
were unimportant. But we can choose to embrace a biblical paradigm, viewing things as they truly are. When we do this, we
realize some things really aren't as important as we thought they
were and other things such as people and our relationship with
Christ are more so. We are wise to hold the things of this world
(jobs, vehicles, promotions, Super Bowl outcomes . . . our smartphones) with a loose grip and treat the eternal as eternal by

putting our hearts and all the freight of our hopes in his promises—*daily* committing to follow him.

FOR FURTHER REFLECTION

1. Was your transition to Christianity a Copernican shift or more of a gradual change? If you have not yet committed yourself to live as part of God's story, answer this question instead: What kind of change do you think there would be in your life if you placed your trust in Jesus Christ?

2. Why do people who come to trust Christ with their lives sometimes seem to be living nothing like the Bible says Christians should live? Why do faithful, fervent believers sometimes turn into complacent, lukewarm churchgoers? How can this happen?

3. Examine your life. What promises do you see yourself clinging to, hoping for, that are probably not able to bear the weight of your hope? What do you hope for that is temporary or unimportant?

Scripture focus. Read Hebrews 11. Do an Internet search of some of the characters mentioned to learn about their lives. What traits are common among them? How different is the way the people in Hebrews 11 viewed life from how most people you know view life? In what way?

Practice. Are there promises that God would have you hope in that you don't give much thought to? Consider doing an Internet search for promises of God. Write down a few that are meaningful to you, and put them somewhere you will see them regularly.

Defining Life Backwards

Life can only be understood backwards;
but it must be lived forwards.

SØREN KIERKEGAARD

One of the primary reasons it's so difficult to maintain an eternal paradigm is because we don't really think much about eternity or how to prepare for it. Having only a tenuous grasp on what we think eternity might be, we plan for the trip but not for the destination. How different would our lives be if we planned them with the end in mind?

THE JOURNEY AND THE DESTINY

Suppose a man is moving from Dallas to Atlanta, where he'll spend the remaining fifty years or so of his life. He plans every meticulous detail of the two-day drive: what he'll wear, his rest stops, where he'll eat, where he'll get gas, where he'll spend the night. But when he arrives in Atlanta, he has no idea what he's going to do. We recognize that this is absurd, but what we understand to be palpably absurd on this level is not so evidently absurd to people looking into eternity. In this analogy, the two-day drive is a clear metaphor for our time here on earth, and the fifty years in Atlanta our eternal destiny.

What is obvious in the physical realm is not so obvious in the spiritual. Why are we not much bothered by our lack of regard for the future? We plan, engage and pursue our various activities with tremendous relish. We even write purpose statements for our businesses, but few of us write purpose statements for our lives.

Our present condition is very real, and our current activities demand our attention. But this is a passing age—whole cultures, civilizations and indeed the whole world will have been gone long before we experience even the beginning of the fullness of our eternity. The fact is that we will last forever, and the things that we see before us now will depart. This one fact changes everything, setting us in an entirely different context.

In *The Weight of Glory*, C. S. Lewis says:

> It is a serious thing to live in a society of possible gods and goddesses, to remember that the dullest and most uninteresting person you talk to may one day be a creature which, if you saw it now, you would be strongly tempted to worship, or else a horror and a corruption such as you now meet, if at all, only in a nightmare. All day long we are, in some degree, helping each other to one or the other of these destinations. . . . It is with the awe and the circumspection proper to them, that we should conduct all our dealings with one another, all friendships, all loves, all play, all politics. There are no *ordinary* people. You have never talked to a mere mortal. Nations, cultures, arts, civilisations—these are mortal, and their life is to ours as the life of a gnat. But it is immortals whom we joke with, work with, marry, snub

and exploit—immortal horrors or everlasting splendours. This does not mean that we are to be perpetually solemn. We must play. But our merriment must be of that kind . . . which exists between people who have, from the outset, taken each other seriously. . . . And our charity must be a real and costly love, with deep feeling for the sins in spite of which we love the sinner.[1]

We are all immortal creatures, destined either to live an eternal, resurrected existence with Jesus Christ or destined to successfully avoid God and his claims and live in a Christ-less eternity. These are our only options. And this truth should make a tremendous difference in the way we plan and live our lives.

Lewis also said, "Christianity is a statement which, if false, is of *no* importance, and if true, of infinite importance. The one thing it cannot be is moderately important."[2] But that's what most churchgoers choose, isn't it? Most people choose the third option, the one that is really no option at all. We regard the truths of Christianity as moderately important. The fact is, though, that it's either all or nothing, everything or not anything. If this radical stuff is true, then it has the most profound and compelling implications for all of our lives and destinies. A journey is always, necessarily, defined by its destination.

Last Words

W. C. Fields was known to regularly mock the city of his birth, Philadelphia. In a 1925 *Vanity Fair* article, Fields wrote his own mock epitaph: "I'd rather be in Philadelphia." Another story about him says that he was caught reading the Bible near the time of his death. When asked about it, Fields responded, "I'm looking for loopholes."

P. T. Barnum's last words were evidence that his focus did not extend beyond his deathbed: "How were the receipts today at Madison Square Garden?" Talk about a guy who never got the point of life! Facing eternity, he's still checking his wallet!

The words a person utters on his or her deathbed, whether believer in Christ or nonbeliever, demonstrate his or her perspective. Contrast Fields's last words with those of D. L. Moody, one of the world's greatest evangelists who preached for forty years, founded three Christian schools and inspired many preachers after him. Sometime before his death, he said:

> Some day you will read in the papers that D. L. Moody, of East Northfield, is dead. Don't you believe a word of it! At that moment I shall be more alive than I am now; I shall have gone up higher, that is all; out of this old clay tenement into a house that is immortal—a body that death cannot touch; that sin cannot taint; a body fashioned like unto His glorious body.[3]

After a restless night just before his death, Moody said, "Earth recedes; Heaven opens before me!" When his son assumed his father was asleep and dreaming, Moody responded, "No, this is no dream. . . . It is beautiful. It is like a trance. If this is death, it is sweet. There is no valley here. God is calling me, and I must go."[4]

Wrestling with the Tough Questions

I had a terrifying experience when I was nineteen years old. I had a whole big weekend planned, but for various reasons the whole thing fell apart, and I found myself alone in my fraternity house. The break from my frenetic activity forced me to focus on the big questions of life. Where am I? Where did I come from? Why am I here? Where am I going? I was terrified because I had no answers.

And, having no answers, I promised I'd be sure that I would never leave myself without something to do again. Like so many others of our time, keeping busy became my way of avoiding the fundamental issues of life.

It reminds me of filmmakers such as Ingmar Bergman and Woody Allen. Both of their early films focused on the fundamental questions of life: love, God and death—painful questions for them. Bergman went through one film after another, exploring the apparent meaninglessness of life without God. *The Seventh Seal* from 1957 is a tremendous example of this in which a medieval knight plays a game of chess with Death and loses. But a turning point came after 1968's *Hour of the Wolf*, when Bergman seemed to no longer wrestle with those questions. His films became psychological instead of metaphysical because a person can only wrestle with life's hard questions out of a context of unbelief for so long. Eventually, it becomes too painful—even unlivable.

Woody Allen was indirectly mentored by Bergman and followed the same path. Initially, he dealt with love and death (he even made a 1975 film with this name) and the issues of purpose and meaning in life. Then, after 1989's *Crimes and Misdemeanors*, the metaphysically oriented films ceased, and the films became purely psychological.

You can only live without real hope for so long before you'll have to manufacture some kind of a false optimism in order to go on. You cannot live for long without some kind of hope, even if it's not founded in reality, because it is a necessity for life. The worth of that hope, though, will become more obvious the closer to the end you are.

ENTERING OUR STORY

In his 1973 book *Breakfast of Champions*, Kurt Vonnegut— who had turned fifty and was wrestling with the issue of his own mortality—put one of his characters through something quite unusual.

Vonnegut shows up at the end of his own novel, driving a Plymouth Duster that he's rented from Avis. From inside his Duster, he gets the attention of his character Kilgore Trout. Then he says: "Mr. Trout, you have nothing to fear. I bring you tidings of great joy. . . . I am a novelist, and I created you for use in my books." Vonnegut promises him a Nobel Peace Prize and offers to answer any questions.

Trout asks if the author is crazy. Vonnegut says no and then says about Trout, "I shattered his power to doubt me." Vonnegut transports Trout to "the Taj Majal and then to Venice and then to Dar es Salaam and then to the surface of the Sun, where the flames could not consume him—and then back to Midland City again." Trout crashes to his knees.

Vonnegut tells his character:

> I'm approaching my fiftieth birthday, Mr. Trout. . . . I am cleansing and renewing myself for the very different sorts of years to come. Under similar spiritual conditions, Count Tolstoy freed his serfs, Thomas Jefferson freed his slaves. I'm going to set at liberty all the literary characters who have served me so loyally during my writing career. You are the only one I am telling. For the others, tonight will be a night like any other night. Arise, Mr. Trout. You are free. You are *free*.

The shaking Trout rises to his feet and Vonnegut wishes him "Bon voyage." As Vonnegut disappears, he hears Trout calling in his father's voice, "Make me young, make me young, make me young!" Those are the last words of the novel.[5]

Now stop and think how you might feel if you discovered you had just been used by some novelist and that was the only purpose for your life. You'd fall into despair. In fact, the worldview that Vonnegut communicates by his writings is one in which life is utterly absurd.

The contrast between this and the truth couldn't be more startling. God also enters into his creation. The author does come. However, instead of telling us we were created for someone's entertainment, he says, "I created you for intimacy with myself, and I want you to experience true reality." By entering into our world instead of showing off, he became one of us; and he now identifies with our experiences in solidarity with the human condition. He says he wants to be with us, not for a few days, but forever. He wants intimacy with us forever (see Revelation 21). *That* is what the author of *our* story wants for us. He sets us free, not to wander without a script but to enjoy life and live it to the fullest, in intimate relationship with the author who created us.

There are several ways we can determine value and significance. One measure is longevity. If something is only beneficial for a period of time, it may be good but not that good. The fact that the work of Shakespeare—or the Bible, for that matter—has survived as long as it has (and remains good) proves something about the worth of Shakespeare and the Bible. The question of longevity can also help with worldviews. There has always been something innate in us that causes us to want to believe in something that lasts, giving proof to Ecclesiastes 3:11—that God has set eternity in our hearts.

This is why Vonnegut's Trout cries out, "Make me young, make me young, make me young!" We all want to be young forever. This is part of the good news: Scripture tells us we will be. Our resurrected bodies will not age. We will not die or get sick or experience death again. God says, "I am making everything new!" (Revelation 21:5). That's the reality that we embrace when we set our story in his context. That is what gives us hope.

Contrast Vonnegut's dismal ending with a believer's fictional account of the end. In the final chapter of his book *The Last Battle*, C. S. Lewis tells of a conversation between Aslan (the lion who sang the mythical world of Narnia into being) and the children who helped him save a Narnia-gone-bad. Lewis writes:

> Aslan turned to them and said:
> "You do not yet look as happy as I mean you to be."
> Lucy said, "We're so afraid of being sent away, Aslan. And you have sent us back into our own world so often."
> "No fear of that," said Aslan. "Have you not guessed?"
> Their hearts leaped and a wild hope rose within them.
> "There was a real railway accident," said Aslan softly. "Your father and mother and all of you are—as you used to call it in the Shadow-Lands—dead. The term is over: the holidays have begun. The dream is ended: this is the morning."
> And as He spoke He no longer looked to them like a lion; but the things that began to happen after that were so great and beautiful that I cannot write them. And for us this is the end of all the stories, and we can most truly say that they all lived happily ever after. But for them it was only the beginning of the real story. All their life in this world and all their adventures in Narnia had only been the cover and title page: now at last they were beginning Chapter One of the Great Story, which no one on earth has read: which goes on forever: in which every chapter is better than the one before.[6]

The end of Narnia is a reflection of what the end will be like for us. Lewis's portrayal demonstrates hope, a radically different paradigm than is demonstrated by the hopeless and broken figure of Vonnegut's Trout.

Broken Stories in the Context of Eternity

All of us have broken stories: shattered dreams, failed plans or squashed hope. For most of us, life isn't what we thought it would be like when we were younger. Even when we are young, there are disappointments. People have let us down. Our careers aren't everything we wished they would be. We have financial setbacks, health problems, relational difficulties and alienation. All of us have experienced shattered dreams; that's the nature of our earthly life.

We need not despair, though, if we are followers of Christ. God has a way of repairing the broken stories of this fallen but temporary world. History will reach a denouement. We are moving toward a grand climax in which all will be well. We are moving toward the beginning of something that will last forever in which every day is better than the day before. We will continue to grow in our emotions, intellect and knowledge of who God is. We will never be able to plumb the depths of the mystery of God, and therefore we will never be bored. Scripture invites us to believe that somehow we'll recognize each other. We'll be radically different in ways we cannot even begin to imagine (1 John 3:2). We'll see each other glorified (as God now sees us). As Paul says in 2 Corinthians 5, we will not look at anyone according to the flesh. We'll see them in a new way, in a different light, as immortal beings.

The things we declare now to be important about a person—his position, her wealth, where she lives, what he drives—these will all be insignificant. Socioeconomics, race, status—all these things are trivial. The things that cause us to have real solidarity with one another are a common destiny, a common Lord and a common life. Our commonality gives us far more dignity and far more identity than any of these surface things that we use to try to position people. None of those matter in light of eternity.

Don't confuse this world with home. Most of us live with more comfort and more prosperity than kings lived with as recently as two centuries ago, and in our unparalleled affluence there is danger. The more prosperous we are in this world, the harder it will be for us to live as if this world is only a passing thing. The more we clutch it, the greater its hold on us. And we can find ourselves clinging tenaciously to position and possessions that take hold of our hearts and lead us to confuse the temporal and eternal perspectives yet again.

Very often, it takes what author Sheldon Vanauken called the "severe mercy" of God to bring us down to the point of absolute desperation and break us. Only then are we made aware of our desperate condition and lack of control. Only then will we be willing to receive the good news of Christ. Until then, it's not good news. We don't seek out good news when we're feeling fine. So our broken stories become the perfect places for Jesus to enter our lives.

Please heed this warning: even *after* you come to faith in Christ, you're not nearly as likely to be dependent upon him and radical in your trust if things are going well for you. This is when you most need to be cautious and ask him to help you love him even more than you love the good things in your life.

There's nothing wrong with prosperity. God is not opposed to wealth. But he is opposed to you being consumed by your wealth through it taking your heart. Hold to the things of this world with a loose grip because, eventually, those things will be someone else's anyway. You'll leave everything behind.

PLANNING

Like the man driving from Dallas to Atlanta, some of us plan for a two-week vacation better than we plan for the rest of our lives because we understand that our vacation's destination determines the journey. But isn't this even more true for our lives? Søren Kierkegaard had a great idea: define your life backwards and then live it forward; determine at the outset where you want to be at the end of your journey. Stephen R. Covey, author of *The 7 Habits of Highly Effective People,* says that most successful people make a practice of beginning with the end in mind.

Imagine your earthly life is over. You have nothing but memories behind you and the grave in front of you. Now ask yourself, "What would it take for me to look back over my shoulder to my past and say that I lived a satisfied life?"

With the answer to that question you can plan your journey, preparing with the end in view. Certainly, this is preferable to just hopping in the car. While people have done it ("Come on, kids, get in the car. We're going on a two-week vacation. We have no idea where we're going, but it's going to be great!"), it's a gamble. And there's a big difference between gambling with the next two weeks and gambling with the rest of your life.

Why do so many people engage in this lack of planning without seeing the absurdity in it? I believe it's because our destiny and purpose seem so vague and frail to us. We give orthodox opinions about eternity. We claim to believe there really is a heaven and a hell. We know that time on this earth is brief, but our so-called beliefs have little bearing on the way we actually live. All of it seems so far in the future that we mistakenly act as if it's not really there at all. We can lull ourselves into a false sense of security in this world when we act as if what we do on this planet won't have any bearing on eternity. Scripture invites us to see it otherwise.

What might a life look like if it were defined backwards and lived forward? First, we must know what our purpose is. The Westminster Shorter Catechism starts by defining life backwards with this question: "What is the chief end of man?" The answer: "Man's chief end is to glorify God, and to enjoy him forever." You can't ask for a better start than that. But certainly we can add more specifics. We can remember the things that God says will last: his Word and relationships. The more we love and serve others in Christ, the richer our relational rewards. And just as there is continuity between earthly and heavenly relationships with the people of God, so those who cultivate a growing appetite for the experiential knowledge of God in this life will presumably know him better in the next life than those who kept God in the periphery of their earthly interests. There can be no more compelling reason to maintain an eternal perspective in this life than to know that perspective relates to our future capacity to see God. In light of this desired destiny, we can live every day forward as we press on toward that goal (Philippians 3:13-14).

Renewing Your Mind with the End in Mind

If we want to maintain an eternal perspective, we should not take lightly the admonition to "be transformed by the renewing of your mind" (Romans 12:2). With truth from Scripture and reinforcement through relationships with other children of Christ's kingdom, we can both define and maintain our perspective more easily. Our study of Scripture and our exposure to its message will sustain us. Unfortunately very few people—even Christians—are exposed to the Bible on a regular basis. A commitment is necessary, and we must not lose our perspective by ignoring or discounting the importance of God's Word. Something powerful happens in our lives when we immerse ourselves in Scripture.

When I seek and pursue and am reminded of the things that last, I can remember that I too am destined to last. If I lose sight of my purpose and destiny, then the eternal perspective will become very remote. This is the ongoing battle that we can expect to encounter for the remainder of our days because this struggle between the visible and invisible never goes away.

READING THE BIBLE BACKWARDS

When the followers of Jesus Christ lose their interest
in heaven they will no longer be happy Christians and
when they are no longer happy Christians they cannot
be a powerful force in a sad and sinful world.

A. W. TOZER

Who doesn't want to be happy? And if the same pursuit that brings us happiness also transforms us into the powerful force in this world mentioned by Tozer,[7] why would we not do it? Why would we not focus on heaven as a regular practice?

Theologian Wayne Grudem says, "We must not lose sight of the fact that Scripture consistently portrays this new creation as a place of great beauty and joy."[8] There will be no more crying or mourning (Revelation 21:4). We will see "the glory of God, and its brilliance was like that of a very precious jewel" (Revelation 21:11). There will be no evil there or any lies (Revelation 21:27). We will reign forever (Revelation 22:5). But above all these things, we will enjoy unhindered fellowship with God. "Look! God's dwelling place is now among the people, and he will dwell with them. They will be his people, and God himself will be with them and be their God. 'He will wipe every tear from their eyes'" (Revelation 21:3-4).

In *Bible Doctrine*, Grudem says:

In the Old Testament, when the glory of God filled the temple, the priests were unable to stand and minister

(2 Chron 5:14). In the New Testament, when the glory of God surrounded the shepherds in the fields outside Bethlehem "they were filled with fear" (Luke 2:9). But here in the heavenly city we will be able to endure the power and holiness of the presence of God's glory, for we will live *continually* in the atmosphere of the glory of God.[9]

To be sure, there will be singing and rejoicing and worship, the kind of worship we have only experienced traces of on earth, during which we've realized it is "our highest joy to be giving him glory."[10] In that heavenly city, this joy will be enhanced as we are surrounded by mighty armies of heaven, friends who have welcomed us and the tangible presence of God himself. The joy will no longer be fleeting. We will be with him forever and in his presence "there is fullness of joy . . . [and] pleasures forevermore" (Psalm 16:11 ESV).

There is a goal great enough to keep all of us driving forward.

FOR FURTHER REFLECTION

1. In what way does your story change if eternity is your ultimate destination? What would it take for you, at the end of life, to look back over your shoulder and say that you had lived a satisfied life? With the answer to that question, imagine what you would need to change in your life. What would you need to begin doing now to be able to look back and feel you had lived well? Are there plans you need to change or new plans you need to implement? Write your answer or discuss it with someone else.

2. Consider this text from the chapter: "All of it seems so far in the future that we mistakenly act as if it's not really there at all." Does eternity seem too far away for you to think about? What can you do now to be preparing yourself for where you live forever?

3. Read the quote from A. W. Tozer, who said that Christians who have lost their hope of heaven are no longer happy Christians and cannot be a powerful force in the world. How interested in heaven are you? Would you say you are a "happy Christian"?

Scripture focus. Spend some time thinking about Romans 12:2. Start practicing it. How will you begin to renew your mind and align your thinking with God's? Spend some today searching out Scriptures about renewing your mind. Consider an online search of what God says about himself or what God says about our thinking.

Practice. If you chose to view everyone as C. S. Lewis explains—as immortal creatures, destined either to live an eternal, resurrected existence with Jesus Christ or destined to live in a Christ-less eternity—how would that change your interactions with people? Copy the whole Lewis quote on a card. Read it every time you'll be encountering other people—at the beginning of the day, as you leave your office, when you go to the gym, and so on. Try to practice seeing people in this way.

Trusting Eternity
or Cursing Time

For time is like a fashionable host
That slightly shakes his parting guest by the hand,
And with his arms outstretch'd, as he would fly,
Grasps in the comer; welcome ever smiles,
And farewell goes out sighing. O, let not virtue seek
Remuneration for the thing it was!
For beauty, wit,
High birth, vigour of bone, desert in service,
Love, friendship, charity, are subjects all
To envious and calumniating time.

WILLIAM SHAKESPEARE,
TROILUS AND CRESSIDA

—⟋⟍—

Time passes, whether we like it or not. We can choose to view it as Shakespeare does here[1]—two-faced and "calumniating" (lying, making false accusations against us to ruin our reputations)—or we can accept it as our inescapable companion

in this life. The story in which we have set our lives and the perspective we take (temporal or eternal) will determine how we
view and are affected by the passing of time.

The eternal perspective asks us to "number our days, that we
may gain a heart of wisdom" (Psalm 90:12). With that heart of
wisdom, we will make decisions to serve God and treasure the
time he's given us. We become more intentional, more aware of
our destinies, and we value time as currency that we invest in
people who will last eternally.

On the flip side of this, we see people who have tried to ignore
time and define their purpose as they go. Yogi Berra once said,
"You've got to be very careful if you don't know where you are
going, because you might not get there." By choosing not to
choose, where do you end up? Where is "there"? The temporal
perspective tells us there is nothing beyond this world. It offers
no hope, and it is out of this lack of hope (or out of a manufac-
tured false hope) that people who fail to choose an eternal perspective will view time and approach people.

Conclusions

Throughout history, we see many great thought leaders become
discouraged as they get older because they near end of their lives
and still have not found the answers they spent their lives
seeking. Socrates, who devoted his life to seeking truth and died
several hundred years before the birth of Christ, had this to say
while he awaited execution: "All of the wisdom of this world is
but a tiny raft upon which we must set sail when we leave this
earth. If only there was a firmer foundation upon which to sail,
perhaps some divine word." These are sad words from perhaps
the greatest thinker of his time.

Socrates longed for more than he had found in a lifetime of
learning; he thought he might find some "divine word" and was,

interestingly, executed on the grounds that he was looking for "new deities." Of course, our view as Christians is that there is a deity greater than the Greek gods of Socrates's time and that the "divine word" was revealed on this earth after the great philosopher's death.

Napoleon said before his death:

> I die before my time, and my body shall be given back to the earth and devoured by worms. What an abysmal gulf between my deep miseries and the eternal kingdom of Christ. I marvel that, whereas the ambitious dreams of myself and [my contemporaries] should have vanished into thin air, a Judean peasant, Jesus, should be able to stretch his hand across the centuries, and control the destinies of men and nations. I know men; and I tell you that Jesus Christ is no mere man. Between Him and every other person in the world there is no possible term of comparison. . . . I myself have founded empires; but upon what do these creatures of our genius depend? Upon force. Jesus alone founded His empire upon love; and to this very day millions would die for Him.[2]

Aldous Huxley, author of *Brave New World*, also gave his life to study and writing. He began as a humanist, but his widely varied interests led him later to spiritual subjects, specifically eastern mysticism and experimental drug use. Though he was unable speak on the day of his death, these are some of his last words: "It is a bit embarrassing to have been concerned with the human problem all one's life and find at the end that one has no more to offer by way of advice than 'Try to be a little kinder.'"[3] In other words, after a life of studying from a temporal perspective, all this man—considered one of the sharpest minds of his time— could offer was a platitude. In 1963, in the terminal phases of throat cancer, Huxley instructed his wife to inject him with LSD and he died.

Sigmund Freud's final words are sadder still: "The meager satisfaction that [man] can extract from reality leaves him starving."[4] That's an intriguing but depressing statement, and yet most people who have studied Freud's life would not be surprised.

Armand Nicholi, a professor of psychiatry at Harvard Medical School, contrasted the worldviews of C. S. Lewis and Sigmund Freud, studying each of their works and correspondence in his book *The Question of God*.[5] Reaching the end of the book, it becomes clear that Freud's worldview led him to total despair. It also had a profound impact on his relationships with others as it made him very self-centered and resignedly morbid. Lewis's theism had the opposite effect on him. Volumes of Lewis's correspondence with people he cared about have been published and continue to be a source of encouragement to others decades later.

SHORT-SIGHTED INTELLECTUALISM

The philosophies of those who have chosen a temporal perspective have frequently led them not to value time and people but to see both in terms of their utility. The book *Intellectuals* by Paul Johnson[6] described and contrasted a number of people who were known to be thought leaders and major shapers of our culture: Karl Marx, Sigmund Freud, Heinrich Ibsen, Jean Jacques Rousseau and others. Interestingly, the common denominator among these great thinkers was that they were in love with the ideal of humanity but really hated people. Johnson carefully demonstrates the fact that every one of them used and tossed away the people in their lives when those people no longer seemed useful to them.

Marx was a prime example of this. He had a theory of the working proletariat (working-class people) and carried some emotion and passion for them as a subject. But he never knew a single one. It was all theory, never practice. As Christians we're called to love real people, not some flimsy ideal of humanity. There's a fundamental difference. We're called to love the people in our presence, in our path, in our lives. We're even called to love the ones who aren't useful to us—perhaps especially these.

The lives of the people in Johnson's book demonstrate how we are affected by our view of our destiny. Whether we choose a temporal or eternal perspective will determine whether we reach the end of our journeys starving for satisfaction and cursing "calumniating time" or possessing a wise heart and eternally valuable relationships. The decision is ours to make, and it demands to be made.

TIME AND WORLDVIEWS

Three worldviews vie for our allegiance in our present world, yet only one of them leads to an eternal perspective. It would be wise for us to gain a basic understanding of them.

The first worldview claims that ultimate reality is material, and everything in the universe is the impersonal product of time and chance. There are variations of this view, but it is best known as naturalism, atheism or humanism. In the end, it promises total annihilation. When we die, we simply cease to be.

The second worldview claims that ultimate reality is not material but spiritual. However, in this context "spiritual" is not a personal being but the mysterious all-that-is. Variations of this view include monism, pantheism, transcendentalism and the New Age movement. Its promised end is reincarnation. But before we begin to entertain ideas about the wonderful possibility of starting over again and making it out better on the second go around, we need to understand something. Contrary to the popular version of reincarnation in the West, the religions of the East teach that reincarnation is undesirable since it brings us around and around on the painful wheel of life. Someone who really believes in reincarnation does not want to wake up and find that he has failed so badly in life that he has to do it again. The Eastern vision of salvation is absorption into the ocean of being, not a vision of personal consciousness or eternal relationships but instead a spiritual version of annihilation.

Theism, the third worldview, distinguishes between the creation and the creator and declares that ultimate reality is an infinite, intelligent and personal being. Christian theism affirms that this personal God has decisively revealed himself in the person and work of Jesus Christ. Only this third worldview offers genuine hope beyond the grave. The Bible teaches that we will be resurrected into an eternally new existence of light, life and love characterized by intimacy with God and with one another. While we don't know every detail about heaven, we believe that everything we go through now will be more than worth it in the end (2 Corinthians 4:17). The divine architect of the universe, the God and Father of our Lord Jesus Christ, has promised to welcome us into that eternity.

IMMORTALITY AND TRANSFORMATION

In an attempt to discount the hope of eternity, some humanists have actually made a philosophical argument against the soul's immortality that runs this way: if our souls really were eternal, life would be a hell of absolute and infinite boredom. Bernard Williams's essay "The Makropulos Case: Reflections on the Tedium of Immortality" is based on a play in which the lead character, Elina Makropulos, is given an immortality serum and remains at the apparent age of 43 though she is actually 342 years old. Elina is bored, indifferent, cold and joyless. Williams sees Elina's condition as an unavoidable consequence of living too long. He believes that eternal life would inevitably lead to an endless "tedium" of life unchanged.[7]

Williams's hypothesis actually reveals more about his deficiency of imagination than it does about the immortality of the soul. We will not be bored in heaven because God is infinite and will always be filled with surprises. Frankly, the more we study nature, the more mysterious and extraordinary it becomes. We may deduce that the same will be true of heaven.

The people of God and the Word of God will endure. We will go on into eternity; we will be the inhabitants of the new heavens and the new earth, and we will not be bored. Williams assumes that to live forever would be to live unchanged, but followers of Christ are always in process. We cannot deny time. Our bodies are wearing out fast, but the apostle Paul gives us hope: "We do not lose heart. Though outwardly we are wasting away, yet inwardly we are being renewed day by day" (2 Corinthians 4:16). The body will perish, but that which is going on into eternity is being renewed and developed every day of the rest of our earthly lives.

We already have manifest in us the life of the kingdom that is to come. In Christ, we are already new creations (2 Corinthians 5:17). We are not who we once were. From the inside out, we are being transformed. Our deepest selves partake of the divine nature; the life of Christ is in our life, and the spirit of God is in our spirit (2 Peter 1:4). Now, this process—bringing our outward selves into conformity with what we've become on the inside—becomes our greatest call in life.

I'm more and more impressed by the depth of the Christian vision as opposed to the shallowness of alternative views. Naturalism says that ultimate reality is simply material; the new age says that ultimate reality comes as some force, energy, vibration or consciousness. The Christian vision is deeper than both of these because the God of our vision and his wisdom have no end. Throw away the idea of an eternity of choir practice and harp music (unless, of course, those are your favorite things) and imagine an eternity of all people growing into the fullness of who they were intended to be—an eternity where we don't start from scratch but continue into better and more fulfilling relationships with our loved ones and our Creator. God promises a new heaven and a new and perfected earth, so it is probable we will never run out of things to explore. We will learn, grow and never be bored. I assure you of this.

TIME—FRIEND OR FOE

A. W. Tozer died the same year as Aldous Huxley, but the life he lived had been entirely different. His life was marked by a "long obedience in the same direction."[8] He became a believer in an infinite, personal God at the age of seventeen and stayed his course. He believed that life on this earth is a short preamble to something far better and that our lives and physical bodies give evidence to this fact. He said:

> The days of the years of our lives are few, and swifter than a weaver's shuttle. Life is a short and fevered rehearsal for a concert we cannot stay to give. Just when we appear to have attained some proficiency we are forced to lay our instruments down. There is simply not time enough to think, to become, to perform what the constitution of our natures indicates we are capable of.[9]

An eternal perspective tells us that we were meant for far more than this creation can offer. C. S. Lewis said: "If I find in myself a desire which no experience in this world can satisfy, the most probable explanation is that I was made for another world."[10] We come to the realization that we have longings that can never be sustained, satisfied or fulfilled in this world. These aspirations cannot be satisfied by any of the offerings of a transitory world because there's not enough time. There's not enough opportunity or energy on this planet even to scratch the surface of our deep-seated, God-given hopes and dreams.

God has implanted eternity in our hearts (according to Ecclesiastes 3:11), and we cannot eradicate the desire for eternity. It's hardwired. We can try to avoid it by indifference and distraction. But it's always going to be there, gnawing away at the earthly prospects that seem so promising but end up having no value or no power whatsoever. God has planted deep longings within us, and if we are wise we will allow these to become magnets that draw our hearts to the only realm in which these longings will be satisfied.

For those disappointed by this world and this life, this is all very good news.

Tozer beautifully gives his answer to the problem of the short duration of our earthly lives:

> How completely satisfying to turn from our limitations to a God who has none. Eternal years lie in His heart. For Him time does not pass, it remains; and those who are in Christ share with Him all the riches of limitless time and endless years. God never hurries. There are no deadlines against which He must work. Only to know this is to quiet our spirits and relax our nerves. For those out of Christ, time is a devouring beast; before the sons of the new creation time crouches and purrs and licks their hands.[11]

The concert is ahead. When it arrives, it will be glorious because it will be unsullied by human ambition, double-mindedness, pride, vanity and foolishness. All that will be done away with, and the body of Christ, cell by cell, will be restored into the perfection that has really been God's intention all along. Spots, wrinkles and all other such things will be removed so that it will be holy, blameless and pure.

Now imagine what that concert will be like when all that is best in us is brought out and all that was wrong in us is decisively removed. Even one hour in that experience—of the true communion of the saints (not to mention the presence of the Lord God whom we will see face to face)—would be more than anything we can imagine. The experience of joy in heaven is something we could not sustain here. We would be disintegrated, undone. No one can look upon God and live now. But in the next life, the Bible says we will "see his face" (Revelation 22:4). We who were banished from the garden and from God's manifest presence will live in the city of God and see him face to face.

DISSOLUTION OF THE GREAT GLOBE

One of William Shakespeare's last plays, *The Tempest,* is about a magician named Prospero who uses his magic books to rule an enchanted island. He fills it with spirits and beings that serve him. Near the end of the play when Prospero addresses his guest Ferdinand, it is as though Shakespeare himself is speaking his parting words to the audience at the Globe Theatre:

> Our revels now are ended. These our actors,
> As I foretold you, were all spirits and
> Are melted into air, into thin air:
> And, like the baseless fabric of this vision,
> The cloud-capp'd towers, the gorgeous palaces,
> The solemn temples, the great globe itself,
> Yea, all which it inherit, shall dissolve
> And, like this insubstantial pageant faded,
> Leave not a rack behind. We are such stuff

As dreams are made on, and our little life
Is rounded with a sleep.[12]

At the end of the play, Prospero gives up his magic and turns his thoughts to the grave. In his final work, Shakespeare showed that the temporal achievements and accomplishments of humanity would all come to an end.

It's reminiscent of 2 Peter 3:10, which gives us a vision of a fiery consumption of all human attainments on the day of God. Peter says, "The day of the Lord will come like a thief. The heavens will disappear with a roar; the elements will be destroyed by fire, and the earth and everything in it will be laid bare." All that we see—this "theatre of life," the "great globe itself"—will dissolve. It will fade and "leave not a rack behind."

TIME TELLS OF THE POWER AND CREATIVITY OF GOD

I took a photo of a dandelion that turned out extraordinarily well, and it's now on my desktop. I like it so much because it's a reminder of how easy it is for us to overlook the brilliance and creativity of God. We'll see thousands of these little flowers turned to puffballs in our lifetime. As children, we might wish on them and watch all the little seeds scatter. My photo caught this one at the point when it was a perfect sphere. Its structure was marvelous, crafted beautifully to reproduce, with white fluff around each seed perfectly suited as a parachute to carry the seeds great distances. The dandelion is absolutely exquisite in its complexity, simplicity and beauty and yet profound in the information that is contained within it. And this elegant, aesthetically pleasing thing is only one weed on the surface of God's creation.

This is what God's fallen creation looks like. What do you suppose his new creation will look like when we and our earth are restored to the condition we were in before there was sin? The

Bible says that no eye has seen, no ear has heard—our hearts have not even an idea of what God has prepared for us who love him. We do not yet have sufficient cognitive ability to understand or embrace it, but the story will continue, and time will tell.

Time will tell also of the contrast between the power of men and the power of God. Imagine the apostle Paul as he stood before Nero. The first time Paul was brought to Roman imprisonment, he was acquitted. This time, he wouldn't be. His last letters (1 and 2 Timothy and Titus) demonstrate his awareness: "For I am already being poured out like a drink offering, and the time for my departure is near. I have fought the good fight, I have finished the race, I have kept the faith" (2 Timothy 4:6-7). In other words: "I *know* I'm at the end of my journey." This small man stood in chains before a powerful emperor, Nero. Imagine what the great emperor must have looked like with his splendor and pageantry. Imagine Paul in his chains and poverty. At that time, one might have supposed that future generations would want to emulate the great Nero. One might suppose that history would pity Paul. It's interesting that two thousand years later, we name our children Paul and name our dogs Nero. (When we live within God's story, things that aren't right can change.)

All the pomp and splendor of man is nothing in comparison with the power of a life transformed by the indwelling spirit of God. There is a new power and dimension in him that the world does not understand. Jesus standing before Pilate in John 18 is a perfect example of that. The powerful Pilate asks, "What is truth?" even though the incarnation of truth was standing right in front of him! It seems that Pilate was actually frightened by Jesus. "Who are you?" he asked. He knew he was dealing with someone extraordinary. Now, besides Bible readers, who remembers the name Pilate? Time exposes what will last and what will not.

Treasuring Time and People

Not too long ago, I spoke at a retreat near Baton Rouge. Some of the men at the retreat were people I'd known for years, and I really treasure the unity of spirit I felt there. Some of us were gathered around talking after the Friday night session, and the conversation was glorious. A friend of mine brought out six rare bottles of wine, among them a 1976 Chateau Lafite Rothschild. When he shared the wine with us, my friend said, "I want to enjoy it now with my friends rather than die and leave it behind." I asked him to write down the names of the wines. I wanted to remember them, for the sake of the moment. It was a magical four hours in the presence of people I loved, enjoying the goodness of God's creation, and I will never forget it. But even at the time, I was thinking that this was a gift to my memory, something that I could look back on forever. We want to hold on to these moments, but we know that we cannot even while they're happening. There's something about time that makes you want to stop it. You want to hold on to it, and yet it slips through your fingers.

Waking Ned Devine is a clever film about a man from a tiny Irish village of about fifty-two inhabitants, all mostly honest Irish country folk living simple lives.[13] Big news hits when they discover that someone from their village has won the lottery. The only problem is that winner Ned Devine lives alone, has no family and got so excited about winning that he died smiling, with his hand still on the ticket. When his friends Jackie O'Shea and Michael O'Sullivan discover Ned and his winning ticket, they concoct a quick plan to keep the winnings from reverting back to the state.

They convince the village to go along with a scheme in which O'Sullivan pretends to be Devine, and it goes off without a hitch when the lottery inspector comes to confirm the winning ticket.

After they believe the inspector has left, the people gather together to remember Devine. The inspector hears singing and
enters the church to see what's going on. O'Shea quickly devises
another plan and begins a eulogy to his friend O'Sullivan, who
is actually sitting in the front row.

O'Shea has the unique opportunity to give a funeral oration
for a man still living:

> Michael O'Sullivan was my great friend, but I don't ever
> remember telling him that. The words that are spoken at a
> funeral are spoken too late for the man that is dead. . . .
> Michael and I grew old together. But at times when we
> laughed, we grew younger. If he were here now, if he could
> hear what I say, I'd congratulate him on being a great man
> and thank him for being a friend.

Why *do* we wait until funerals to speak our love, gratitude and
affection? Why do we reserve our best words for people after their
death? It doesn't make sense. What a wonderful thing it would be
to visit your own funeral, like Michael O'Sullivan, to sit and listen.

An eternal perspective teaches us that relationships can be
forever and that time is not to be feared. Funerals are not the
time for our words of praise—*now* is. If we really believe this, we
will treat people differently. We will remember how many times
the Bible tells us God loves us and wants us to love each other.
We will be generous with our words of praise and more cautious
with our criticism. We will strive to speak words filled with a
divine kindness, spent on people who are God's eternal treasure.

FOR FURTHER REFLECTION

1. How do you feel about the passing of time in your own life?
   Think about how you feel about your birthdays. What kinds
   of issues do they bring to mind?

2. The eternal perspective asks us to "number our days, that we may gain a heart of wisdom" (Psalm 90:12). If that heart of wisdom leads us to serve God and treasure the time he's given us, what does this chapter say will happen? Do you agree?

3. From an eternal perspective, how is time like currency?

4. Yogi Berra said, "You've got to be very careful if you don't know where you are going, because you might not get there." What will happen if you make no plans for the future?

5. Compare the apostle Paul's view to Bernard Williams's. What is the difference in a nutshell? Which perspective is more like your own?

Scripture focus. Write down 2 Corinthians 4:16. Keep it with you. Consider memorizing it. Do you feel your inner self being renewed day by day? If not, consider asking God to make more obvious to you how he is changing you for eternity.

Practice. C. S. Lewis said: "If I find in myself a desire which no experience in this world can satisfy, the most probable explanation is that I was made for another world."[14] Ask God to reveal your true desires, the things which the world cannot fulfill for you. (Write them down if you like.) Ask God to give you the assurance that these longings are signs of his eternal plans for you.

Poets, Saints and Heroes

*Be very careful, then, how you
live—not as unwise but as wise, making
the most of every opportunity, because the days
are evil. Therefore do not be foolish, but
understand what the Lord's will is.*

Ephesians 5:15-17

Have you ever had a hero, someone who saved the day? Was it Luke Skywalker? Superman? Harry Potter? There is something about hero stories that rings with truth because it seems that the darkest hour is the point at which a great transformation takes place. One hero, a little hobbit, made a big difference to his friends and to his world. His name is Samwise Gamgee.

In the 2002 movie adaptation of J. R. R. Tolkien's *The Two Towers*, two heroes, Frodo and Sam, are in a desperate situation. Their quest to prevent an evil ring from falling into the hands of a dark lord seems lost. As a battle between the forces of good and evil rages around them, Sam and Frodo have lost contact with the other companions from their quest.

Frodo, losing hope, fears the task at hand is too much for him. He tells Sam, "I can't do this." But Sam, through the simplicity of faith, recalls his own childhood heroes as he encourages Frodo to carry on:

I know . . . I know. It's all wrong. By rights we shouldn't even be here, but we are. It's like in the great stories, Mr. Frodo. The ones that really mattered. Full of darkness and danger they were, and sometimes you didn't want to know the end, because how could the end be happy? How could the world go back to the way it was when so much bad happened? But in the end, it's only a passing thing.[1]

It is times like these that make a hero great. Sam, the humble, everyman character, is bold here by encouraging Frodo to continue. Through that straightforwardness of faith and the quest for his purpose, he carries on in spite of great odds.

It is my belief that the greatest heroes, men and women, have not been recorded in church history books since the inception of the church. The vast majority of those people were, like Sam, of modest means—unsung heroes of the faith who pressed on in those dark hours. They weren't really noticeable, yet they clung to the hope that God had given them. They would not make a mark on this world visible to humans, but they knew that God had called them for a purpose. Size had nothing to do with the importance of that purpose. These aren't people who gave in or begged God to make life go their way; they instead persevered in their trials knowing that what was in store for them was much better than any wish they could ever dream.

We can look at the small spot we occupy on this earth inside this enormous galaxy in our unimaginably large universe and be overwhelmed with awe or even fear. But our size seldom has anything to do with our importance. Just ask Samwise Gamgee.

THE PARABLE OF THE SHIP

In some respects, it's easy to see that we are on a planet that may be in its darkest hour. There *is* a dark lord that threatens us. Yet instead of persevering in hope, it's easy for us to fail to hear the messages; life in the immediate is *so loud.* "Now" can be so overwhelmingly frightening or painful that we lose our long-term perspective and become incapable of hearing any voice of warning or wisdom. *Or* "now" can be so enjoyable and compelling that we become distracted from our eternal perspective and begin to lay our hope on things that cannot bear its weight. I once heard a pastor tell a story that illustrates this well:

A luxury liner was traveling across the Atlantic as a massive party took place in its ballroom while a storm raged outside. As a result of the storm, an accident occurred, leaving the ship critically damaged. But the people were unaware of the damage, and the captain (seeing that everyone was having such a great time drinking and dancing) didn't believe the reports and didn't allow notice of the accident to be broadcast over the speakers. So the party and the journey (and the storm) continued.

Eventually, a warning was issued: "The ship is fatally damaged; you must come to the lifeboats." It blared over the PA system and rescuers shouted the message to individual passengers. But most of the people were caught up in the festivities. The band played loudly as the ship was sinking, and the people were really enjoying themselves. The few who ventured out did notice that the ship actually *was* leaning toward the starboard side.

Interestingly, some of the people became confused. They put on their lifejackets, but the party had been so much fun that they went back to try to squeeze in a few more minutes.

Others rushed past the rescue workers to their quarters. Once inside their cabins, they were gripped with fear of what was now a clear reality. Some began to fall down and pray. "God, something is terribly wrong. We will follow you . . . if you will please just stop our ship from going under." But it became evident that he wasn't changing his plans. So they got up off the floor and returned to the ballroom. When asked where they had gone, their reply was that they had believed the earlier report. They had prayed to God, and it didn't work.

So the ship eventually sank. Right before the final plunge, there was a last-minute rush to the lifeboats and frantic searching for life vests. But the boats were gone, and there were no more life vests. No comments were heard about continuing the party as the ship was engulfed by the rolling waves.[2]

Those who embraced life in the ballroom lost their lives, while those who heeded the warning and boarded the lifeboats lived. But there is a second story here, the story of those who, even in a time when they were totally powerless and most in need of help from an all-powerful saving force, demanded that God change *his* plan. When those people returned to the ballroom, they would see that ballroom life had lost something, but refusing to be saved, they, nonetheless, lost their lives. The only people who would be saved were the ones who heeded the message and stepped out into the unknown *lifeboat life*. They would save their lives and eventually enter into a new life, valuing the second chance at life they'd been given.

How many times are we hanging onto something we know won't last because we're afraid to step out into the unknown? How many others of us can look back and remember the moment at which we were saved, the turning point that has brought us to a much better place? As we dig deeper into developing an eternal perspective, it becomes clear that it's not going to be easy; it's not a one-time decision. There will be times when we hurt so much that we might prefer the distraction of a ballroom, and there will be times that are so good that we find ourselves praying to God to let us stay there. We will be forced to make our choice again: *either we will view all of our life in light of the eternal, or we will cling to the temporal, trying to modify the eternal to conform to our desires.*

The latter is a terrible blunder. It's foolishness to try to persuade God to modify his great plan only to get on board with your personal agenda, but there are many who try to do this. They're not interested in lifeboat life, but they unwittingly allow themselves to be lured into the water by the sirens that call them to their deaths.

Heavenly Minded in the Present Tense

In Thornton Wilder's *Our Town*, after Emily has died she's allowed to go back and observe a single day of her brief life. The stage manager, her guide, advises her, "Choose the least important day of your life; it will be important enough." She makes the mistake of choosing her twelfth birthday. And she is so overwhelmed by the experience that she concludes:

> I can't! I can't go on! It goes so fast. We don't have time to look at one another. I didn't *realize*. So *all* that was going on, and we never noticed! Take me back—up the hill—to my grave, but first: wait! One more look. Goodbye! Goodbye world. Goodbye Grover's Corners, Mama and Papa, goodbye to clocks ticking and my butternut tree and Mama's sunflowers, and food and coffee and new ironed

dresses and hot baths and sleeping and waking up. Oh earth! You're too wonderful for anybody to realize you!

She looks to the stage manager through her tears. "Do any human beings ever realize life while they live it?" The stage manager answers, "No. Saints and poets, maybe. They do some."[3]

But how do you live with care and live the present to the full, knowing the days are evil? The apostle Paul advises: "Be very careful, then, how you live—not as unwise but as wise, making the most of every opportunity, because the days are evil" (Ephesians 5:15-16).

It is sometimes said that a person can become "so heavenly minded that they are of no earthly good." I do not believe this is so. People who develop an eternal perspective place value on the present, treasuring the passing opportunities of this life and becoming more alive to the moment, not less. They're not looking ahead to what they can gain or accomplish but are savoring everything for what it is. From this perspective, we aren't overwhelmed by the pain of this life or seeking to avoid it. Instead we begin to understand that it will pass and that enduring brings great reward. As Paul says in Romans 8:18, "Our present sufferings are not worth comparing with the glory that will be revealed in us."

Paul knew something about suffering. After living a life of outrageous faith, he was beheaded just outside of Rome in AD 67. In a letter to his young friend Timothy, he says, "For I am already being poured out like a drink offering, and the time for my departure is near. I have fought the good fight, I have finished the race, I have kept the faith" (2 Timothy 4:6-7).

We all want to finish well, but we never will unless we're willing to fix "our eyes on Jesus, the pioneer and perfecter of faith. For the joy set before him he endured the cross, scorning its shame, and sat down at the right hand of the throne of God" (Hebrews 12:2). Paul said there was waiting for him a "crown of righteousness, which the Lord, the righteous Judge, will award to me on that day—and not only to me, but also to all who have longed for his appearing" (2 Timothy 4:8). And we are those who long for his appearing, or at least we are becoming them.

This kind of kingdom living is upside down according to the world's point of view. So while we live here, our faith leads us to accept a great deal of paradox: we've got to lose our lives to save them and be last in order to be first. We must die in order to live and serve in order to lead. We are strongest when we are weak, and we're weak when we think we're strong. We died in Christ, but we've never before been so alive. To grow wiser, we must become like children. While we are walking on earth, we are also citizens in heaven. We should love this earthly country but not love the things in it. We are sinners but also saints. In our flesh is no good thing, but we are cleansed from sin. We are the reason why Christ died, yet we are the apple of his eye. We fear God, but he is our comfort. We're overwhelmed by his presence but drawn to be close to him. We love supremely one whom we've never seen. The powers of darkness are vanquished by Christ, but the final conquest is in the future. When this life is over, we expect to live forever.

And here's one of the biggest paradoxes of the Christian faith, one that I have not seen many in Christendom embrace: *being* is more important than *doing* and must precede it. Oswald Chambers said in *My Utmost for His Highest* that we count as service what we do for Christ, but he counts as service who we are to him. If our focus is on who we are and who we belong to, the doing will follow. I'm convinced that being (living in intimate relationship with God now) should precede all that we do and become our empowering force. "But whoever looks intently into the perfect law that gives freedom, and continues in it—not forgetting what they have heard, but doing it—they will be blessed in what they do" (James 1:25). *We can't have the doing without the being.* This applies to every component of our lives.

If we seek his kingdom first, he promises the rest of our needs will be supplied (Matthew 6:33). But if we instead pursue only the work of our hands, we craft a false self based upon doing and having. Intimacy will energize and empower our activity, but activity will not necessarily lead to intimacy. Christian philosopher Blaise Pascal said that our biggest problem is that we don't know how to sit quietly in a room. We cannot stand being still. This is what retreats are about—being somewhere in solitude, away from smartphones, computers and even books. If we choose to invest in solitude and be alone with God in the present, we would probably learn more about ourselves than we could in a year of activity.

THE PARABLE OF THE STONE

It is easier to become a Christian if one is not a
Christian than to become a Christian if
one is already supposed to be one.

SØREN KIERKEGAARD[4]

In his last book, *Attack Upon "Christendom,"* nineteenth-century Danish philosopher Søren Kierkegaard denounced the declaration from the state Lutheran church that all Danes were born Lutherans and were therefore Christians. Kierkegaard said there was a radical difference between Christendom (those born into a "Christian" nation) and Christianity (true faith). An external Christianity does not reflect the gospel at all. In Kierkegaard's desire to get people's attention, he said that one must cease being a "Christian" in order to really become a Christian. If we are Christians by birth or by going through the motions, we are not Christians by our will, not to mention by our broken will. Kierkegaard made his point by using strongly provocative language and through stories.

One of these stories, titled "An Eternity in Which to Repent," is a parable about a poor, elderly couple contemplating how they will live out the rest of their days without starving to death. They often pray to God about the matter, and one day there came what seemed to be a solution. That morning when the wife went out to the oven, she found a very large and precious stone on the hearth. She brought it to her husband, and he concurred that they were now set for life. But, pious as they were and seeing that they already had enough to live at least one more day, they decided to wait until the following day to sell the jewel.

That night in a dream, the woman was transported into paradise. There amid all the glories that she could behold was a great hall. The hall was full of chairs that were adorned with beautiful stones. An angel showed the woman to her chair, which was dazzling. However, as she looked at the chair more closely, she realized something was missing. There was a hole in the back of it about the size of the stone she had found on her hearth. When she asked the angel about the hole, he said, "That was the precious stone you found on the hearth. You received it in advance, and so it cannot be inserted again." The woman woke up and told her husband about the dream. Together, the couple agreed that it would be better to continue to trust in God for what they needed to live rather than sell the precious stone. They decided to ask God if he would return the stone to where it came from. That evening, they bravely laid the stone out on the hearth and asked him to take it back. In the morning, sure enough, it had vanished, and they were quite sure of where it had gone.

These two elderly people were happily married, and this woman was sensible. Still, Kierkegaard said, "Everyone has within himself that which more artfully and more urgently and more persistently than any woman is able to make a man forget the eternal and lead him to measure falsely, as if a few years, or ten years, or forty years, were a prodigiously long time, so that even eternity becomes something very short in comparison."[5]

I think this is what many of us do. We frequently act and invest our days and years as if our satisfaction with life here were what mattered most and as if eternity were not a prodigiously long time. Kierkegaard's words shake the complacent Christian:

> You may perhaps be cunning enough to avoid suffering and adversity in this life, you may perhaps be clever enough to evade ruin and ridicule and instead enjoy all the earth's goods, and you may perhaps be fooled into the vain delusion that you are on the right path just because you have won worldly benefits, but beware, you will have an eternity in which to repent! An eternity in which to repent that you failed to invest your life upon that which lasts: to love God in truth, come what may, with the consequence that in this life you will suffer under the hands of men.[6]

If we want to distort the message of Christianity, we can choose to go through life this way. We can be Christians with a temporal paradigm, professing Christians but practical atheists; however, the result of that choice will be that we are seduced by the wrong voices. We will measure our years here as if they were a long time and eternity as if it were nothing. Our lives will reflect this decision. In the end, we will have earned for ourselves "an eternity in which to repent."

However, if we are committed to Christ, we *cannot* behave as if our Christianity is of "moderate importance." As C. S. Lewis said, if it is true, then it is infinitely important, and our lives ought to reflect this belief. Unfortunately, the average churchgoer is a person who seeks to make Christianity moderately important; that is to say, he may fail to see the obvious implications of what this means for eternity.

If we really trust Jesus, we are assured that we will have trouble (John 16:33) and that the world is going to hate us (John 15:19; 1 John 3:13). We must practice our faith every day, expecting that Jesus' promises are true, both the ones we look forward to and the ones we find most difficult. This day could be our last. We are in a battle. The dark lord is here and works among us. We must pick up a sword, expect to battle and die. God has not promised to make us comfortable, but he has promised to forge a Christlike character in us (1 Corinthians 1:8; Philippians 1:6), and he has promised that now is not the whole story.

FACETING

God sees each of our lives like a treasure, like a gem. He desires to separate the gem from the material in which it was found, clean off the debris and polish it. Still, an amorphous stone is not brilliant. Faceting is the process by which the jeweler cuts his stones. The more of these facets, the more beautiful a stone becomes. But imagine being that stone! If God makes us beautiful by a faceting process, we have to imagine there will be quite a bit of pain involved. After the faceting, though, we become brilliant, and like any good jeweler, God sets us in a black velvet background to show contrast.

We live in that black velvet background now. We're a "warped and crooked generation," in which we must "shine . . . like stars in the sky"; we do this by refusing to grumble and complain so that we may become "blameless and pure, 'children of God without fault'" (Philippians 2:14-15). I believe this may be even more necessary today than it was when it was written. God's people are like stars in that black background, gems that God has crafted. And, through pain, he's polished us and faceted us so that we are constantly becoming more brilliant. This is how he mediates his incarnational presence through his people, and this is why perseverance is essential.

Holding On

Let's revisit Frodo and Sam on their quest. As far as they are concerned, all hope is lost. Even while Sam boldly reminds Frodo of those heroes in stories that "really mattered," Frodo battles with his own desire to keep the ring. But unbeknownst to either character, while Sam speaks in faith, their fate actually reverses. Hopeless situations are transformed. The great wizard Gandalf returns with help for their companions to win the battle. Sam continues, unaware of his companions' victory:

> This shadow, even darkness, must pass. A new day will come, and when the sun shines, it'll shine out the clearer. Those are the stories that stayed with you, that meant something, even if you were too small to understand why. But I think, Mr. Frodo, I do understand. I know now, folk in those stories had lots of chances of turning back, only they didn't. They kept going because they were holding on to something.[7]

A shipload of people dances while their destinies are played out in the icy water of the Atlantic. A wise woman almost trades her heavenly treasure for a few more meals. A ring-bearer tries to hold on to what he must not.

What are we most interested in holding on to? Our happiness or our holiness? Our comfort or our character? We know well in which God is interested. So we struggle. We're not home yet, and this is painfully obvious. But in seeking to relieve that pain, we must not deceive ourselves into supposing that this world is enough or even close to enough to heal it or that this world can sustain the deepest longings of our lives because it never will. Do we have the courage to step out and appreciate what seems insignificant over the great celebrations that seem more significant than they are, to hold on to something not-so-tangible?

When the question is asked, "Do any human beings ever realize life while they live it?" I hope our stage manager answers, "Yes, my children do. They are poets, saints and heroes. They understand. They will have chances to turn back, but they won't." And even as he speaks these words, our deserved fate reverses. Victory is ours. And while he is in the midst of his triumph, we continue in our most joyous moments and in our darkest hours, often unaware. But that is just fine. We keep going because we're holding on to something.

FOR FURTHER REFLECTION

1. Who do you know who might be a hero in God's eyes but is virtually unnoticed by the world? Write a few words about that person, or even better, write a letter to encourage him or her.

2. In the parable of the ship, the passengers were distracted by the fun of the party in the ballroom. List the things that keep you from finding solitude and time alone with God.

3. Hearing the call to the lifeboats, what one thing might hold you back? What should you do about it? What is *lifeboat life* for you? What would it look like if you stepped out and away from whatever your sinking ship is and into where you know you are supposed to head?

4. Think of a time in your life when you had the opportunity to
   choose between your happiness and your holiness. What
   drove your decision? Would you choose differently if you had
   the same opportunity again?

Scripture focus. Read Philippians 1:6. Write it down or work
on memorizing it. You can memorize by writing the verse over
and over, by looking at one word at a time, by reading it forward
and backward, by saying it aloud to someone else, or by writing
it down, cutting up the words of the sentence and trying to arrange them in order again. There are many ways to practice
Scripture memorization. As with any muscle, the more you
work, the better you will become.

Practice. Consider committing time this week to *being* instead of *doing.* Spend time sitting quietly, listening to God. Take
a passage or just a phrase or word from Scripture into your time.
Take nothing else, not your phone or a book or your computer.
Arrange to not be interrupted. This is not time for Bible study or
Scripture memorization. Instead, use the time to just *be* alone
with God. When your mind wanders, think about that word
from Scripture to bring yourself back.

Inside Out, Upside Down
and Talking to Ourselves

—𝕞—

I n the 2002 movie adaptation of J. R. R. Tolkien's *The Two Towers*, a character named Gollum fights an internal battle that we all face. Gollum was once the owner of a magical evil ring that has a powerful attraction but leads to the corruption of anyone that bears it, and Gollum loved and bore the ring for too long. The story's hero, Frodo, extends unlikely compassion to Gollum by asking for his help to destroy the ring. This tears at Gollum, though, as he begins to struggle between what he knows is right and what he craves.

Before he found the ring, Gollum was a regular hobbit named Sméagol. But his desire for the ring and his envy of anyone else that possesses it has degraded him both internally and externally into the most pitiful creature of Middle Earth, so much so that he no longer bears any resemblance to what he once was. His only desire is for his "precious" ring, and he is accustomed now to living in caves and shadows. Yet Gollum is invited by Frodo to step out in a grand adventure of serving a higher purpose. In essence, Frodo invites him to live in a greater story.

Throughout the journey, Gollum feels severe internal conflict. But the spirit of Sméagol returns to life when Frodo reminds Gollum of his real name. He gains a renewed sense of identity. The transforming creature pledges his allegiance to Frodo and serves his new master as a scout and provider of food.

As this renewed nature emerges, Sméagol's dark side wrestles for dominion. In a key scene of self-confrontation, his evil self commands him to betray his new master. Instead of submitting, Sméagol fights back. There is no longer a need to trust in his own trickery to survive because as he tells his dark side, "Master [Frodo] looks after us now."

The conversation intensifies as Sméagol and Gollum argue. Finally, the dark side wields its mightiest weapon, reminding Sméagol of his shameful past and murderous acts. Backed into a corner, Sméagol leans on faith in his new master and coura- geously says to his evil side: "Leave now . . . and never come back." This is a defining moment for Gollum/Sméagol as all power is suddenly drained from his evil side. Realizing this new authority and liberation, Sméagol cries again with louder confidence, "Leave now and never come back!"[1]

This is our battle too: who we've been versus who we are be- coming, our old story versus our new one, who we are now versus who we are committed to be. It's a battle of belief and commitment. It's a battle that, for most of us, rages regularly in our own minds and requires our "holding on to things [our] reason has once accepted, in spite of [our] changing moods."[2] It is discipline in our minds. It's heeding the Holy Spirit's whisper and the mention of his seal upon us that marks us as God's pos- sessions. Only by persistence in these things are the loud accusa- tions of our enemy silenced. It is a risk like the one Sméagol took, based on faith in our new story and the faith that "Master looks after us now."

Upside Down

> *Who is wise and understanding among you? Let them show*
> *it by their good life, by deeds done in the humility that*
> *comes from wisdom. But if you harbor bitter envy and*
> *selfish ambition in your hearts, do not boast about it or*
> *deny the truth. Such "wisdom" does not come down from*
> *heaven but is earthly, unspiritual, demonic. For where you*
> *have envy and selfish ambition, there you find disorder and*
> *every evil practice.*
>
> *But the wisdom that comes from heaven is first of all*
> *pure; then peace-loving, considerate, submissive, full of*
> *mercy and good fruit, impartial and sincere.*
>
> James 3:13-17

Committing to an eternal worldview involves tremendous risk, personal discipline and powerful hope. It is so countercultural that it often leads to a feeling of estrangement among our peers and can leave us wondering if we've made the right choice. But life lived by this worldview produces positive outcomes in the here and now, not just in the future. It leads to good behavior, gentleness, mercy, sincerity and ultimately to peace. It fosters the growth of even greater hope. These can ultimately counter the estrangement we may have to endure for a time.

The value system that comes from below is the world's system. It is a temporal, bottom-up system, and it requires no risk. If we believe in only what we see and that this world is all there is, it's from this world that we must extract all of our happiness, hope, purpose and sense of accomplishment. We must seek fulfillment in the present tense. If this is all there is, "let us eat and drink, for tomorrow we die" (1 Corinthians 15:32). It requires no trust and demands no dependence, and it doesn't sound too bad . . . at least at first. But once this wisdom has a hold on us, it's hard to get free. The results of this kind of wisdom are selfishness, jealousy and disorder. Its end is ugly and evil. We don't see this until we can't get free, but it is a bondage that can send us straight into despair because by *not* hoping in Jesus, we're forced to put our hope somewhere else on something that looks precious but will ultimately degrade us.

The apostle James stayed focused on seeing things from heaven's perspective, emphasizing the importance of remaining dependent on and submitted to God. James addressed practical problems that his recipients were well aware of, specifically that their faith was not manifest in their decision making. Maybe this is why he asks, "What causes fights and quarrels among you? Don't they come from your desires that battle within you?" (James 4:1).

He says that the other wisdom (that which does not come from God) is "earthly, unspiritual, demonic" (James 3:15). These are hard words. There is no middle-of-the-road wisdom, some way that's not God's way but isn't all that bad. Earthly wisdom is (like it or not) of the devil. Satan is the ruler of this world, inspiring its systems and worldview to be opposed to God. This is what is meant by spiritual warfare. We fight against Satan, the one behind the lie that the visible world is more authentic than the hidden one and that what we see is all there is (or at least superior to what is not seen). It's an old lie. He used it on Eve in the Garden of Eden to separate her from God and man, and he'll use it on you to do the same. Any wisdom in this world that is not God's is a threat to our relationship with him. That's why James says, "Anyone who chooses to be a friend of the world becomes an enemy of God" (James 4:4).

Simply put, you can't play by two sets of rules. You need to discern your *ultimate allegiance*. It's not wrong to engage in business and make a profit, and it's not wrong to plan and prosper and enjoy your life. But you mustn't be presumptuous in your plans about the future. And you must always be on the lookout for the dangerous signs of jealousy, bitterness, selfish ambition and arrogance, knowing that they produce disorder and every evil thing. All of these danger signs are internal things, but they shape our behavior and demonstrate to which worldview we really adhere.

You have the choice to put away the evil in your life, beginning with your thoughts. And you can choose to "accept the word planted in you, which can save you" (James 1:21) in the same way. This leads to a regenerate mind; then at least some of our thoughts will become like his thoughts and our will can begin to move into alignment with his. But if we allow this bottom-up system to affect our thinking, our minds can end up fixing on our own will, which is opposed to God. Our own desires will conceive and grow, leading ultimately to death and separation.

THE GESTATION OF SIN

When tempted, no one should say, "God is tempting me." For God cannot be tempted by evil, nor does he tempt anyone; but each person is tempted when they are dragged away by their own evil desire and enticed. Then, after desire has conceived, it gives birth to sin; and sin, when it is full-grown, gives birth to death.

Don't be deceived, my dear brothers and sisters. Every good and perfect gift is from above, coming down from the Father of the heavenly lights, who does not change like shifting shadows.

JAMES 1:13-17

In his book *Not the Way It's Supposed to Be,* Cornelius Plantinga discusses the nature of sin itself. Plantinga defines sin as a "culpable disturbance of shalom."[3] What a perceptive insight. Sin disturbs the harmony of who we truly are. Shalom is about more than just peace. It's about unity and our rhythm with God. When people are in shalom with one another and with God, there is a convergence of authenticity. Anything that disrupts this is sin. This fits well with what James says about shalom coming from above. In fact, we cannot create this kind of peace and instead are called to preserve it (Ephesians 4:3). The evil from below is the thing that disturbs it.

Even Christians experience the temptation to live by a bottom-up system. We live in the world, and none of us are perfectly immune to its influences. The danger signs we just looked at all first appear in the mind and make their way to the heart. They'll likely not be noticeable in you until they've been there long enough to start producing their results.

Notice the process here. This is the gestation of sin: first it is conceived in your mind, then it grows and finally gives birth. And when it gives birth, it gives birth to action. So the sin is the concretized mind, the outcome of the thoughts that we allowed though we knew they were opposed to God. In other words, lust, evil desire—whatever is in your mind—will eventually birth sin if given freedom to grow. What has lived for a time in the mind becomes real in your actions. And when sin is accomplished and it has lived out its course, it brings forth death. In effect, this is the birth of death, and it all starts in your mind.

This is a problem as a growing number of Christian Americans are allowing their thoughts to be guided by culture more than by their own faith systems. In a 2003 study, researchers from The Barna Group found that almost half of the American population held a non-biblical moral view on at least half of the

core behaviors they surveyed.[4] Yet a more recent ABC News/
Beliefnet poll found that roughly 80 percent of Americans claim
to be Christians.[5] How is it possible that most Bible-believing
Christians hold non-biblical perspectives on key moral issues?

TRANSFORMED BY RENEWING OUR MINDS

Your mind holds the key, and Romans 12:2 reminds us that we
are transformed by its renewing. Ironically, though, almost
every sermon I hear says, "This is what you ought to *do*. . . ." We
hear that we ought to live out the faith of Old Testament heroes
or we should do the things that Jesus told us to; our churches
ought to be organized a certain way, and we ought to adhere to
certain practices. But we don't hear very much about how we
ought to *think*, how we should manage our own will or allow
our minds to focus on—*the life that is lived inside our heads
and hearts.*

Our thought life is critical. As a man thinks, so he is (Proverbs
23:7). If we begin with our behavior, we won't necessarily change
our thoughts. Instead, we'll just hang new habits on an old
nature. But if we can get our thought life right, good actions are
likely to emerge from the divine foundation those good thoughts
provide, and our new nature can emerge. The system we're most
familiar with works from the outside in, but the other system
(the one Jesus taught) works from the inside out. It demands that
we start change by considering first what we believe and think
and dwell on. We rarely hear sermons about how to manage
what is floating around in our brains. Without learning and
practicing discipline, we tolerate a great many thoughts that are
not worthy of the person we're called to be.

Living in this backward system as we do (and as we are rarely
admonished *not* to do), we act and then rationalize our actions.
We hear sermons filled with what author Dallas Willard calls

"the gospel of sin management,"[6] and we practice it. We maintain our "personal sin profiles" in such a way as not to cause embarrassment to ourselves or others. We keep our sin low-profile as best we can and only share safe confessions and prayer requests with others.

But your thought life will eventually be birthed into action. One way or another, it's inevitable because the things you think about and allow your heart and mind to dwell on are your meditations. Whether your sin is worry or lust or hatred or envy, what you spend large chunks of time thinking on will eventually change and shape your character.

Our character will eventually expose some of what we've been thinking. It will demonstrate for a watching world whether we are thinking predominantly about sin or if we are rather making every effort to keep God's Word in the forefront of our minds.

Talking to Yourself

*The first step is to recognise the fact that your
moods change. The next is to make sure that, if you
have once accepted Christianity, then some of its main
doctrines shall be deliberately held before
your mind for some time every day.*

C. S. Lewis

In his book *Mere Christianity* Lewis argues that once we've decided to believe in something (based on the evidence *for* it) we must be reminded of that evidence regularly. No belief, Lewis says, will "be deliberately held before your mind"[7] without being fed. This is why disciplines like Scripture reading, prayer and meditation are so important.

But thought life is underplayed in our current American Christian culture. We have so under-stressed the practice of some spiritual disciplines that our wills have grown flabby and weak. We fail to train our minds toward holiness. Instead we just allow them to roam where they will without really making any choices about it.

But there is good news. There is a choice to make. You can choose to *listen* to yourself (follow the thoughts wherever they may lead you) or you can choose to *speak* to yourself (direct where your thoughts go). If you listen to yourself, you'll hear the whining and complaining of your flesh, still full of the old nature's hatred and bitterness. Your flesh will naturally lead you off into all the wrong things. That's *listening* to yourself. You will meditate on something, whether it's something you've chosen or something you've just stumbled on. But you have a choice.

In *speaking* to yourself and *choosing* what you will think about, you can create habits. And those habits, over the course of time, can work toward changing your attitude. It can be possible to think yourself into a new way of doing, and it's possible to put into practice your new way of thinking. Speaking to yourself gives you an opportunity to make a conscious choice.

Do not be anxious about anything, but in every situation, by prayer and petition, with thanksgiving, present your requests to God. And the peace of God, which transcends all understanding, will guard your hearts and your minds in Christ Jesus.

Finally, brothers and sisters, whatever is true, whatever is noble, whatever is right, whatever is pure, whatever is lovely, whatever is admirable—if anything is excellent or praiseworthy—think about such things. Whatever you have learned or received or heard from me, or seen in me—

put it into practice. And the God of peace will be with you. (Philippians 4:6-9)

Notice Paul puts thoughts before actions here, which is important. Rather than downplaying the thought life, Paul speaks to that issue first.

If left to yourself, do you meditate on what's true, honorable, right, pure, lovely, reputable, excellent and praiseworthy? Does your mind gravitate toward those kinds of things? No. No one's mind naturally goes in that direction without practice. If we're not careful, we will end up with our focus on the opposite end of all these godly values. Watch the news or read a newspaper. Those things don't sell by focusing on the true, the good and the beautiful of God's wondrous creation. They sell by titillating and feeding the temptations of our flesh.

Sadly, we are often sloppy with things that matter. We tolerate more than we should and seldom really *practice* self-control. We allow the input of a form of wisdom that is not from God and fail to train our minds in God's wisdom. And this bottom-up system *is* a *form* of wisdom. Just as the serpent in the Garden of Eden was described as more cunning than all the beasts of the field, so is this wisdom shrewd.

And it *has* snuck in. It's been so quiet that we didn't even notice that it was becoming the dominant worldview in our country, even among Christians. In another 2003 survey conducted by The Barna Group, it was revealed that only 4 percent of American adults employed a biblical worldview as the basis for their decision making.[8] Among Christian groups, the figures were only slightly higher, none of them exceeding 13 percent with a biblical worldview.[9] About these findings, George Barna said:

> Our goal should be to act like Jesus. Sadly, few people consistently demonstrate the love, obedience and priorities of

Jesus. The primary reason that people do not act like Jesus is because they do not think like Jesus. . . . Although most people own a Bible and know some of its content, our research found that most Americans have little idea how to integrate core biblical principles to form a unified and meaningful response to the challenges and opportunities of life.[10]

It is important to recognize that worldly wisdom bears no resemblance to the wisdom that accompanies an eternal paradigm. God's wisdom is first holy and pure. It doesn't have any hidden agendas, and it doesn't play by two sets of rules. Søren Kierkegaard said that purity of heart is to will one thing. By practicing this focus of will, speaking to ourselves and training our faith, we gain a heavenly wisdom. That wisdom is "peace-loving, considerate, submissive, full of mercy and good fruit, impartial and sincere" (James 3:17). What you see *is* what you get. It commits to truth and clings to it. This wisdom causes its adherents to keep their promises, even when it hurts.

So as you move toward God and turn away from selfish ambition, you become a renewed person who demonstrates mercy, good fruits and an unwavering desire to avoid hypocrisy. These are the fruits of a thought life that is disciplined and focused on eternity. We make the choice to conquer disorder, jealousy and every evil thing and choose that which produces harmony and peace.

We demolish arguments and every pretension that sets itself up against the knowledge of God, and we take captive every thought to make it obedient to Christ. (2 Corinthians 10:5)

The battle must first be fought in our minds. Of course, other battles will ensue. There will be battles for our affections when what we want challenges what we believe. And there will be battles in practice when we find that acting on our beliefs is more difficult than we had anticipated. But training ourselves in faith, knowing what we believe, and reminding ourselves of the reasons we came to believe in the first place can hold us steady and spur us on. As Lewis points out, it can keep us from being "just a creature dithering to and fro, with its beliefs really dependent on the weather and the state of its digestion. Consequently one must train the habit of Faith."[11]

The Ripple Effect

A friend of mine who owns a construction company (we'll call him Jeff) was involved in bidding on an enormous project that should have resulted in big profits for him. But after he'd committed to the job, he discovered that one of his most trusted employees had made a terrible mistake and submitted a bid that turned out to be outrageously unrealistic. The company had committed to the too-low bid, sure, but who keeps a promise they didn't mean to make? Earthly wisdom would have told Jeff to watch his bank account. There comes a point, however, when we are forced to make a choice between what ultimately serves only us and what serves the one we claim to be serving. Jeff was at that point, and he made his choice.

> Simply let your "Yes" be "Yes," and your "No," "No." Anything more comes from the evil one. (Matthew 5:37, Berean Study Bible)

Jeff completed the project as promised. He did the work for the price on the accepted bid, even though it ended up costing him huge financial loss. He had the option of backing out. There were loopholes. He could have reneged on the arrangement legally if he had wanted to. Yet the words of God that had been planted in his mind and heart now seemed to be speaking back to him. Something within Jeff was saying that he'd made a commitment, and that mattered more than money. It wasn't about his interests but something more.

> May these words of my mouth and this meditation of
>   my heart
> be pleasing in your sight,
> LORD, my Rock and my Redeemer. (Psalm 19:14)

Jeff isn't a perfect person. None of us are. But something happens when the meditation of your heart and mind has an eternal focus. He knew that integrity was critical and an eternal kind of ethics flowed from his eternal focus. He had given his "yes." He kept his promise even when it hurt (Psalm 15:4) because something told him that, all things considered, keeping his word was of a higher importance.

The irony is that sometimes what we lose here on earth provides for gain in eternity. I don't know if Jeff eventually gained back the money he lost on that deal, but I wouldn't be surprised. And I wouldn't be surprised to find there were believers on the other side of the negotiating table afterward because of the courage and faith my friend demonstrated.

When Jeff chose to turn his business decision into a step of faith, something happened. Suddenly, the decision wasn't just about him, his business and the other company. The decision was about the kingdom of God. When he abandoned the desire to do what was right just for his finances and instead acted to keep his promise, a ripple effect was created.

If we train our hearts and minds in the principles of God's eternal wisdom, we will be changed. We will face decisions differently. We may be able to make bold choices like my friend did when opportunities arise, and our actions may ripple into eternity. If we fail to train in faith, that other wisdom will sneak in. It's inevitable. Maybe it already has in your life. But it's not too late. You can face your reflection down and yell at the self-ishness, bitterness and envy you see and demand that it "leave now and never come back!" There is no fear in doing so because Master looks after us now.

FOR FURTHER REFLECTION

1. If you are a *Lord of the Rings* fan, watch the recent movies or read the chapters in the books about Frodo, Sam and Gollum. Note what you see if you think of it as an allegory.

2. What is life like inside your head? What thoughts do you need to weed out? What do you need to feed your mind? How will you do it? When will you start?

3. Read James 1:13-17. The passage says, "Every good and perfect gift is from above, coming down from the Father." These words from the passage are often quoted; however, they're not usually quoted in context. What is the context in the passage you just read? Why does it matter?

4. What is the practical step Lewis gives for maintaining an eternal worldview? How necessary is this practice for being a Christian? How do you feed your belief system?

Scripture focus. James 4:4 says, "You adulterous people, don't you know that friendship with the world means enmity against God? Therefore, anyone who chooses to be a friend of the world becomes an enemy of God." How do you feel about what James is saying? In what ways are you a friend of the world? Be honest with yourself. You're the only one reading this. This chapter talks about putting evil out of our minds, beginning with our thoughts and renewing our minds. Have you ever practiced this or caught a thought that was stirring around in your mind and refused to think about it anymore, replacing it with a truth you know about God from Scripture? This week, take this challenge: memorize some of the Scriptures verses listed below. Use them to renew your mind and fight the temptation to think from a temporal perspective.

- John 15:4

- Ephesians 2:10

- Philippians 1:6

- Philippians 4:19

- James 1:13-17

Practice. Make a plan to begin speaking to yourself this week. What will you do differently? How will you renew your mind and guard your thoughts? Here are some additional Scriptures about renewing your mind:

- 2 Corinthians 10:5

- Deuteronomy 15:9

- Isaiah 55:7

- Matthew 15:19

- 2 Corinthians 4:4

Flight Plans, False Goals and a Life Uncommon

—〰—

In 1938, an Irish-American pilot named Douglas Corrigan flew his jalopy single-engine plane across the Atlantic Ocean by mistake. Or so the story goes. According to his report to authorities at the airport where he landed, he had made a navigational error because of fog and an inability to see his instruments in the dark. He had filed a flight plan that plotted his course from New York to California, but despite being an experienced pilot, he "mistakenly" flew by the wrong end of the compass needle and didn't realize it until it was too late to do anything but land where he was—Ireland. When questioned by officials at the airport near Dublin, Corrigan stuck to his story that the whole thing was just a big blunder. Though Corrigan lost his license to fly, he became a national folk hero upon returning to the United States. For Americans whose spirits had been deflated by the Great Depression, Corrigan's stunt was comic relief.

Although Corrigan never quite admitted it, his "mistake" was likely a ruse to circumvent aviation authorities who had repeatedly rejected his request to make the transatlantic flight to his parents' homeland. The nickname "Wrong Way Corrigan" stuck, and a year later he starred in a biopic about his life (*The Flying Irishman*). We may never know what his intentions were, but his story resonated with the American people who were desperate for a little laugh and maybe even a little taste of courage.

Declared or not, our goals set our course and act as our compass, so we better be sure to choose the right ones. The enticing wisdom of this world bombards us with the message that what we see is all there is and dictates a certain set of goals: maximize your pleasure and minimize your pain, make a name for yourself and gain money, status and power. If you have lived a broken story, you know those goals can lead to disappointment. But wisdom from above tells a different story—that we are immortal creatures and our brief stay on this planet is nothing compared with the eternal existence that awaits us.

The Bible tells us that knowing God is the greatest possible pursuit; he holds in his right hand all we could ever want (Psalm 16:11). Jesus urges us in Matthew 6 to seek his kingdom first and trust that the things we need will be supplied by this same God who knows our needs even before we ask.

But living in this fallen world causes us to easily forget and lose our focus. We get caught in the tension between the goals this world would have us set and the goals we would set if we really believed that what the Bible says is true. This is warfare between an earthly, demonic wisdom and a heavenly, divine wisdom (James 3:13-17), and we're all required to make a choice about which side of the field we are going to play.

While we're deciding, let's look at some of the goals we humans typically seek and try to figure out what's behind them.

FALSE GOAL #1: PLEASURE

Somebody's knockin' should I let him in,
Lord, it's the devil would you look at him.
I've heard about him but I never dreamed,
He'd have blue eyes and blue jeans.

TERRI GIBBS

Ahhh, self-indulgence. Whether it's too much wine, too much ice cream, twenty-eight pairs of Italian leather shoes or too many hits on a website we know we shouldn't visit, when we pursue pleasure as an end in itself, we use the right things in wrong ways and can end up in real bondage. Country singer and songwriter Terri Gibbs broke the bank with her hit single "Somebody's Knockin.'"[1] It spoke to a common temptation for every human being who heard it—sin looks "real good."

Pastor Erwin Lutzer agrees. He says, "Sin never comes to us properly labeled; it always appears wrapped in a different package and presented as something other than what it is."[2] Short-term sensual pleasure can bring long-term pain. Eating and drinking for the wrong reasons can lead to addictions. These top the list but are only a few of the distortions Satan would like to use to trap us. He'd like us to think that the choices are either the pursuit of pleasure or extreme self-denial. But this is all wrong. God isn't trying to keep us from enjoying life. In fact, he wants us to have life in abundance. But real abundance never comes by way of self-indulgence. It comes as a byproduct of seeking the one who holds all of our pleasures in his own right hand—forever.

The wise writer of Proverbs tells us that "whoever loves pleasure will become poor" (Proverbs 21:17). Years later, the apostle Paul passed this same wisdom on to Timothy, saying he counted lovers of pleasure among the people he should avoid (2 Timothy 3:4). And Jesus, the wisest man to ever live, said the pursuit of pleasure can choke out the Word of God like thorns choke out good seeds (Luke 8:14). This pursuit will always disappoint eventually. God has made us for himself, and the deepest pleasure we will ever know is knowing him.

Surely, as Christians, we should be able to see this. So what's wrong with us?

> Why do people who are otherwise so decent, smart, and well-intended—yes, even some committed Christians—behave in ways that are stupid, selfish, and self-destructive? And sometimes evil? Why don't we live up to what we know is right?
>
> The answer, quite frankly, is that we are driven not by reason, but by our desires. We do not behave according to what our mind tells us; we obey our passions that cry out for gratification. To quote the words of Woody Allen (who fell in love with his own stepdaughter), "The heart wants what it wants."[3]

Filmmaker Woody Allen's phrase has become part of our vernacular. Pop star Selena Gomez even wrote a song about it. Obviously, the path of pleasure is not a very difficult one to take. We start down it willfully. But then, as James says, "each person is tempted when they are *dragged away* by their own evil desire and enticed" (James 1:14, emphasis added). We start walking leisurely down an enjoyable path when out of nowhere the snakes of lust and want twist around our ankles and squeeze until we're dead. Usually the path to pleasure is only easy to follow in the outbound direction.

FALSE GOAL #2: APPROVAL

Paul asked a question we should all consider asking ourselves: "Am I now trying to win the approval of human beings, or of God? Or am I trying to please people? If I were still trying to please people, I would not be a servant of Christ" (Galatians 1:10). That's strong language. If I strive to please people, am I no longer Christ's servant?

Let's look to Pontius Pilate for our answer. The governor of Judea at the time of Jesus' death, Pilate was a politician but apparently not a very good one. Assigned the task of ruling over a conquered people who hadn't quite admitted they'd been conquered, Pilate found himself in a very difficult situation that he did not handle well. It appears he was alternately cruel and compromising. Though he is often painted as simply weak, history says Pilate hated the Jews and had a reputation for being brutal and even murderous. His harsh rule had been reported to the emperor, and he was presumably under investigation at the time of the trial of Jesus. Perhaps because of this, on various occasions Pilate would threaten the Jews and make great shows of power to accomplish his purposes, but when the Jews (seemingly not intimidated by these demonstrations) refused to relent, Pilate would concede.

His actions and the well-known question he asked of Jesus in John 18, "What is truth?" help to form a picture of a confused man who made his decisions without consulting any reliable standard. During Pilate's two trials of Jesus, his chief concern as governor should have been dispensing justice. However, it is more likely that Pilate's real interest lay in trying to placate an angry mob while his job as their ruler was on the line. To complicate matters, his wife sends him a message while he's sitting on the judgment seat: "Don't have anything to do with that innocent man" (Matthew 27:19). *Now what does he do?* Pilate symbolically washes his hands and says, "I am innocent of this man's blood" (Matthew 27:24) and sends Jesus to the cross.

Some claim that Pilate later became a Christian, even a martyr. History says he was banished by the emperor Caligula, suffered some kind of breakdown and took his own life. Tragically, Pilate came face to face with the Son of God but was so concerned with the power of the emperor and the power of the mob that he failed to realize that the most powerful figure in history was seated right in front of him, yielding to Pilate's control. Striving to please people took him miles away from a possible relationship with the suffering Messiah whose help he desperately needed.

Missed opportunities and terrible decisions are only some of the consequences we suffer when people's opinions become more important to us than God's. Whether it is recognition that we want or we're just frantically scrambling to avoid consequences, we will ultimately fail when we try to please people. It's God's approval we should seek. The *incidental* outcome of seeking God's approval may be that people esteem us, but it is the goal that matters. We cannot simultaneously seek to be impressive to people and pleasing to Christ.

False Goal #3: Fame

> *Then they said, "Come, let us build ourselves a city,*
> *with a tower that reaches to the heavens, so that we*
> *may make a name for ourselves; otherwise we will*
> *be scattered over the face of the whole earth."*
>
> **Genesis 11:4**

Sounds good, doesn't it? Take a look at Flemish artist Pieter Brueghel's fantastic paintings of the Tower of Babel (figures 3 and 4) to get an idea of what this ziggurat construction must have looked like.[4] These were powerful men building an amazing monument in Genesis 11. It took strong leadership to bring people together for a project of this magnitude, and it took a lot of people working to build one of these things. Who knows how far they got.

Figures 3 and 4. *The Tower of Babel* (one and two) by Renaissance artist Pieter Brueghel

But where was God in the plans of the men who came together at Shinar to make a name for themselves? He was totally missing from their equation. God had told them to spread out and fill the earth (Genesis 9:1). Instead, they huddled up in one place—exactly the opposite of God's instructions. Genesis 11:8 tells us how well their plan worked out for them: "So the LORD scattered them from there over all the earth, and they stopped building the city." The very thing they were working to prevent (obeying the command to spread out) happened in an instant when God came down.

No one wants to leave this earth without making a mark. We all want to accomplish something that will matter and be remembered. And if we are servants of God, it's right to hope we will accomplish something that will last forever. We all ought to fear dying until we have done something that will always live. But it is *how* we go about accomplishing this that matters. In a total inversion of the world's recipe for success, the Bible tells us we ought to humble ourselves, become servants and trust that God will be the one to exalt us (James 4:10). He wants to accomplish great things through us, but he knows that we become proud and set ourselves up for failure when we try to do it on our own.

How difficult is this other way? How hard must it have been for the twelve men sitting with Jesus when he told them, "Anyone who wants to be first must be the very last, and the servant of all" (Mark 9:35). Each one of us has, indeed, been crafted by God to accomplish something that will last forever, but the number one way we are to do this is by investing sacrificially in other people in the name of Jesus Christ.

Jesus knows what works. This becomes more apparent the longer you take him seriously. And he says that if we want to become great, we must become servants. Think about it. If you set your course for fame, it is up to people to determine if you succeed or fail, and people are fickle. Even if you do well, you may not gain their respect. Or you may gain it and lose it as they applaud you one day and turn their back on you the next. Popularity is fleeting.

How popular was Noah? None came with him, except his own family. But to this day, we remember his name because Noah was a servant of God.

In contrast, look at the popularity of the Pharisees. Until Jesus arrived on the scene, they had it all—special seats and special treatment from the people. They had the things that fame can give, but they had nothing of substance. Jesus repeatedly pointed this out. They made a name for themselves, but the lasting reputation they earned was one of disgrace.

Now look at the ridiculed little band of servants from Acts 2 who obeyed Jesus when he told them to go to Jerusalem and wait. They didn't even know what they were waiting for, but they were faithfully praying together when Pentecost happened. The same power that was able to destroy the work and the communication of the men building the tower at Shinar came upon a group of uneducated people who could suddenly speak the language of every pilgrim in Jerusalem. When you read the words of Peter that follow this amazing event, it becomes clear. God was doing for them what the tower people in Genesis 11 wanted to do for themselves. Author Anne-Geri Gray puts it this way:

> Every time I have sought my own gain instead of what is best for the kingdom of God, I have failed. When my hope has been built on my own dreams, I have been paid back in full from their futility.
>
> God has consistently brought down my pride despite the cleverness of my hands (Isaiah 25:11). When one challenges God with a desire for a great-name, God may just take the dare. In any event, the arrogant will be bested in the battle.[5]

God wants our egos to be destroyed so that we can hope in *him*. Any towers on our drawing board without God's supervision and direction are pipe dreams and just dare him to undo them all.[6]

False Goal #4: Wealth

There is nothing on which [the world] is so hard as poverty; and there is nothing it professes to condemn with such severity as the pursuit of wealth!

Ebenezer Scrooge

Like Dickens's English miser Scrooge,[7] Americans love money. We want more of it than we have, and we're willing to do some pretty drastic things to get it. According to authors James Patterson and Peter Kim, 25 percent of Americans would be willing to abandon all of their friends and their church for ten million dollars. For the same amount, 23 percent would be willing to become prostitutes for a week, 16 percent would leave their spouses and 7 percent would kill a stranger.[8] Wow!

Maybe we're not really that bad, but it's tempting to displace our faith with Scrooge's golden idol. The world raises wealth as a standard of success, security and identity, and we buy into it completely. We believe it when we're told that money is sexy and powerful, and we believe wealth can also make us happy and keep us safe. As this temporal value system continues to permeate our culture, this standard becomes a central, driving force in the lives of most people, even those who embrace Christian ideologies. We've gone so far down this road that we can barely see any problem with it.

Our society may be the worst in its focus on riches, but it certainly isn't unique among nations, neither in this age nor in the past. The hunger for wealth is a powerful tool of the enemy; it always has been. The apostle Paul says:

> Those who want to get rich fall into temptation and a trap and into many foolish and harmful desires that plunge people into ruin and destruction. For the love of money is a root of all kinds of evil. Some people, eager for money, have wandered from the faith and pierced themselves with many griefs. (1 Timothy 6:9-10)

The greatest danger related to the love of money is that it pulls us away from faith. C. S. Lewis said:

Prosperity knits a man to the World. He feels that he is "finding his place in it," while really it is finding its place in him. His increasing reputation, his widening circle of acquaintances, his sense of importance, the growing pressure of absorbing and agreeable work, build up in him a sense of being really at home on earth.[9]

If we attain prosperity, the things we are able to purchase may put us at risk of forgetting God. But even if we fail to attain it, we can face the same kinds of problems when we assume that a large bank account will provide for us instead of the one who is always willing to provide for our needs. He only asks that we seek him first.

This doesn't mean that we stop working. Labor is the biblical method for producing prosperity. But again, our focus is important. Who or what are we pursuing first? Are we after wealth, or are we after building a godly character within us? It's not a choice between wealth and integrity. There are wealthy men and women with great integrity. However, there are also many people who sacrifice their integrity to gain wealth, and we must refuse to become like them.

The outcome of our pursuits belongs to God, regardless of what we choose to pursue. If we work with excellence and diligence and let him determine the outcome—that is faith. He may bring a great deal of abundance to one person's life and give very little to another. But what matters is the character you build, not the fortune you amass.

It may be difficult for some of us who are very good at business to accept that God may at times ask us to risk loss in our business when faced with a choice to sacrifice our integrity. We may be offered shortcuts that could produce more profit in less time but that aren't altogether ethical. We will work with greater excellence in the long run if we work as if it were for Christ. We'll avoid the shortcuts. We'll seek out contrast in the gray areas that are causing temptation. We'll boldly refuse to sacrifice our integrity and character to gain wealth and status because wealth and status will never be enough to satisfy. If we chase them, we will eventually find ourselves broken again.

In Luke 12, Jesus tells a parable of man who had arrived at wealth and the good life. After one good crop, the man found himself so far ahead of the game that he could retire.

> Then he [the man] said, "This is what I'll do. I will tear down my barns and build bigger ones, and there I will store my surplus grain. And I'll say to myself, 'You have plenty of grain laid up for many years. Take life easy; eat, drink and be merry.'"
>
> But God said to him, "You fool! This very night your life will be demanded from you. Then who will get what you have prepared for yourself?"
>
> This is how it will be with whoever stores up things for themselves but is not rich toward God. (Luke 12:18-21)

Ouch! And then there's the old Sunday school song about the foolish man who built his house upon the sand "and the rains came tumbling down." Unfortunately, I think I know this person. He is the man who left mission work for oil money and lost his family in the bargain; she is the woman who left her husband for a rich man and forfeited her relationship with God and family; he is the young sales clerk who stored away the petty cash for his own benefit. All of them are broken eventually.

The psalmist said, "Though your riches increase, do not set your heart on them" (Psalm 62:10). We should be happy to set our hearts on relationships that do not cease instead of the golden idol with a temporal life. May we not find, like Scrooge, that we've wasted years on the love of money but instead throw it generously in the right places. *God* is all about generosity, and we who are created in his image should reflect that.

FALSE GOAL #5: POWER

> *Should you then seek great things*
> *for yourself? Do not seek them.*
>
> **JEREMIAH 45:5**

That's a verse we don't often hear quoted. Why? Probably because it is a little too direct. God is the giver of all good things, and if we are going to attain great things, he is the one who is going to make it happen. Period. Sometimes he will grant that great things happen and other times he may show his severe mercy and take our great things away. But our dependence is to be on him. If our goal is to increase our own personal power, then our goal is in conflict with God's.

> In humility value others above yourselves, not looking to your own interests but each of you to the interests of the others. (Philippians 2:3-4)

The Bible is full of specific instruction to walk humbly, humble yourself, practice your humility, pour yourself out, serve others and put others before yourself. The world is going to tell you that this is a waste of time. But the choice is yours.

The thing is, God has actually created in us a *desire* to prosper, but an eternal perspective leads us to give to God the power to prosper us (in *his* time) and to give *our* hearts and *our* energy to things God values. In so doing, we avoid worthless things that will inevitably let us down.

So then what causes us to set our sights on power and status? Look at 1 Peter 5:6-8:

Humble yourselves, therefore, under God's mighty hand, that he may lift you up in due time. Cast all your anxiety on him because he cares for you.

Be alert and of sober mind. Your enemy the devil prowls around like a roaring lion looking for someone to devour.

When Jesus asks us to abandon our own climb to the top and let God be the one to exalt us, he takes away the anxiety along with the responsibility. It may be that we're grasping for power and status because we're afraid. But Jesus says he can handle that. We can let go of this worry. He can take our unease, our fear—and better than that, *he wants to do this.* Jesus isn't afraid of anything.

The quest for power over people is something that some feel driven to pursue. People have killed over the centuries to gain power. They've done horrible things in order to gain something that feels a lot bigger than it actually is. But Jesus, the most powerful person the world had ever known, was the most humble person who walked this planet. He knew that humility is its own kind of power, a mighty form the world cannot understand.

SETTING YOUR FLIGHT PLAN

Small aircraft pilots and charter pilots submit their flight plans to the Flight Service Station (FSS) that services their departure airport, and then the FSS enters the flight plan information into their system. The FSS is responsible for processing flight plans, which include a description of the aircraft, tail numbers, departure and destination airports, flight route, estimated time of departure (ETD), estimated time of arrival (ETA) and the number of people on board. The FSS keeps track of an airplane's

ETA, and the pilot radios in to report the plane's position. If the pilot does not close the flight plan or communicate changes, a search and rescue procedure will be initiated assuming the aircraft to be lost.

False goals lead to being lost. If we submit a flight plan to wisdom, reality and spiritual fulfillment but then instead fly a course to pleasure, recognition, fame, wealth or power, what do we get? A fat lot of nothing. A futile pursuit. A life off course and out of control—Ireland, if you will. We start off heading to the sunny Los Angeles of a life in Christ and end up in the Dublin of disappointment.

Chris Hemsworth, an actor who was named *People* magazine's Sexiest Man Alive, can tell you about fame's disappointments: "You get to Hollywood, you achieve something and then you realize, '[profanity omitted] it didn't actually bring me the happiness I thought it was going to. It didn't fix anything.' . . . I don't wake up, look in the mirror and go, 'Yep, all is perfect.'"

To make matters worse, he says there are incredibly insincere people in Hollywood (big surprise) who years earlier wouldn't even look at him but suddenly were interested after he was famous. "Next time I saw them, they're my best friend. That's gross."[10]

GQ Australia's February 2015 cover features a picture of Hemsworth with these words emblazoned across his chest: "Bow down, for this is the year that our Aussie god ascends on high." But Hemsworth isn't a god, and he knows it. According to the article, he'd rather stay at home with his family than go out and enjoy what fame has earned him. Yet the world has chosen him, helped him reach his goal and then paid him back with paparazzi whose behavior causes him to fear for his children's safety.

False goals like the ones set by Hollywood standards reward with emptiness. Temporal things can't satisfy the human heart; they just leave you craving something else because they're never enough. They'll appoint you a god or kick you to the curb.

Scripture tells us that it's foolishness to put our own pursuits above God's plans for us, but we just keep on doing it. We are not autonomous, and we are fools when we believe we are. An eternal value system, on the other hand, is founded in and remains in *reality*, provides *fulfillment* and leads to *wisdom*. Build a flight plan around those variables and see where you land.

DEPARTURE POINT: REALITY

Many of us have hoped in things that have also died. Death is a harsh fact of life. It comes sneaking up on us with absolutely no warning and can change our reality. What we thought was tangible and constant turns into a memory, leaving us grasping for that person or that dream, so as to make him or it real and living again. With every loss comes another slap in the face from that old enemy, mortality.

From the dawn of time, it has been human nature to want to hold onto life and get the most out of it. The serpent in the Garden of Eden tempted Eve with the lie that life could be controlled, and she took the bait. "If you eat it *now* you will become wise and never die!" This arrogant choice only brought her pain and a deeper understanding of death. Her unhealthy curiosity became her sad reality, and she came to understand what it meant to "pass away."

In 1 John 2:17, John reminds us that many things in this world will pass away and not carry over to the world to come. But the one who does the will of God abides forever. *Our* reality is preparatory to an invisible kingdom that is to come and lasts forever. Understanding the temporal nature of the world will help us live in the reality of it.

Praise be to the God and Father of our Lord Jesus Christ! In his great mercy he has given us new birth into a living hope through the resurrection of Jesus Christ from the dead. (1 Peter 1:3)

This is a living hope that will not die. First of all, this hope is imperishable. Secondly, it's undefiled; it can't be corrupted. Third, it will not fade away. And fourth, it's reserved in heaven for you. *That's* realty. *That's* the thing which will endure forever. Therefore, a man is wise who gives his life in exchange for what God says is permanent and valuable. A man is foolish who trades his life for things God says are despicable and worthless.

CRUISING ALTITUDE: FULFILLMENT

What are the things that people really long for? When they go after people's approval, what do they really want? What do they want from power or control? What drives them, and what do they hope to get? Whether people will admit it or not, all fulfillments in life are summed up with nine surprising words found in Galatians 5:22-23: love, joy, peace, patience, kindness, goodness, faithfulness, gentleness and self-control. It's all there in these fruits of the Spirit.

Look at the list. Even if you just take the first three, they would be enough for most people. Fulfillment is found in love, joy and peace. Many people who seek wealth and power suppose they'll be satisfied when they get them, but neither wealth nor power ever promises to bear fruit. And when we look deep down, we find we desire real things much more anyway. What we really crave is to be loved, to be content and to live in peace with our reality.

SPECIAL EQUIPMENT: WISDOM

A fool finds pleasure in wicked schemes,
but a person of understanding delights in wisdom.

PROVERBS 10:23

Wisdom always relates to skill in the art of living and the ability to maintain every facet of our lives under the dominion of God. The greatest skill that anyone can achieve is the skill of living a godly life. The book of Proverbs, part of what is called "the wisdom literature," discusses all your relationships, how you deal with wealth and the ways in which you speak. Wisdom can inform every component of your life, and it must if you want to live by real moral or ethical standards. But you can only get this wisdom by developing an eternal perspective through the study of Scripture.

Our sin nature drives us to want to have our cake and eat it too. We want the temporal and the eternal at the same time. What we fail to realize is that if we pursue the eternal, the temporal falls into place. While we aren't promised that everything will go our way when we operate from an eternal perspective, we can still taste the fruit, joy and fulfillment while walking in reality. They may not come in the packaging the world promises, but they do come, often in greater measure. If you go for the world first and heaven last, you'll end up missing both. But those who go for heaven first discover joy in this life too, and that is wisdom. Walking in wisdom does not have a thing to do with circumstances but with the understanding of our assurance: we are loved by a real, living God; we have hope and a purpose and a destiny. These things, even one at a time, are worth more than all of the ends of the false goals put together.

DESTINATION: A LIFE UNCOMMON

Jesus' first miracle was performed when he attended a wedding in Cana (John 2). Besides actually turning water to wine, he also performed the miracle of aging it ("but you have saved the best till now," John 2:10). And he made it abundant ("six stone water jars . . . each holding from twenty to thirty gallons," John 2:6).

This story—and the love he showed to this bride and groom—is a picture of his great love for us, an uncommon love that led him to do something exceptional, generous and beautiful.

This uncommon love is also characteristic of the uncommon kind of life he promises us. The world always pours out its best wine first. It knows nothing of saving the best for last. It makes promises and then breaks them when people's discernment has been dulled. We get duped. We think things are what we want, but it later turns out they're not all they're cracked up to be. But God shows his character in the Cana wedding story. He is all about excellence, and anything less wouldn't be a reflection of who he is. The miracle at Cana also reminds us that there is a best reserved for later; the glory of God that we get glimpses of in this life are little sips of what will be poured out in abundance in the life that awaits us.

In light of all this, ask yourself some questions: What will you choose to pursue? Is there something for which you are willing to give your life? To where are you setting your course?

Here's a diagnostic test. If you could be granted one thing, what would it be? Ask and answer it quickly. What comes to mind first? The focus of your heart is far more important than the thing you are trying to achieve.

Everything is spiritual if the focus of your heart is correct. But the skill of living well and living aware of God's presence at all times take practice. We must cultivate it as a skill using whatever methods work for us—set an alarm to remind us to pray, post Scripture on our walls, memorize verses regularly, and so on. But we *must* incorporate these things into our lives. As Deuteronomy 6:6-9 commands, we are to teach the Scriptures to our children, talk about the Word of God in our homes and keep it on our lips and in our hearts. The Word of the Lord is to be the last thing we think upon before sleeping and the first thing on

our lips as we wake. These commands are a reminder to keep
him ever in the forefront. We will be surprised to find that, when
we do, the ordinary takes on a splendor it never had before.

Every day, you will be seduced and pulled by the temptations
of the world system. But if you choose the Word of God and
make it your authority, you will act in a way the world knows
nothing about, and your life will be truly uncommon.

> I used to think—loving life so greatly—
> That to die would be like leaving a party
> before the end.
> Now I know that the party is really happening
> Somewhere else;
> That the light and the music—
> Escaping in snatches to make the pulse beat and the
>   tempo quicken—
> Come from a long way away.
> And I know, too, that when I get there
> The music will never end.[11]

This chapter isn't about dying, and neither is this poem. But it
is about the reality of what followers of Christ are promised will
come. Have you ever lost someone dear to you and then awoken
in the middle of the night remembering the sound of her voice?
It can be disheartening, but it can also be encouraging. Imagine
that voice is beckoning you to get your flight plans in order and
your compass working so that you can stay the course and join
the party waiting for you in heaven. It may sound too good to be
true, but we're promised that it will be good beyond our wildest
imaginings (1 Corinthians 2:9).

Many false goals and temptations will come knocking at our
door. But extended immersion in God's Word will help us develop an eternal value system. This can be our source of fulfillment

and lead us to godly wisdom. It can help us gain the strength to slam the door on the snakes of lust and want, to reject Pilate's hand-washing basin of public approval, to stop building towers with our own blueprints and to lead, God help us all, a life uncommon.

FOR FURTHER REFLECTION

1. Paul asked a question we should all consider asking ourselves: "Am I now trying to win the approval of human beings, or of God? Or am I trying to please people? If I were still trying to please people, I would not be a servant of Christ" (Galatians 1:10). That's strong language. If I strive to please people, why can't I be Christ's servant?

2. What would be an example of pleasing people instead of God, something that might likely happen with you or someone you know?

3. Have you felt the pleasure of knowing God or of being right where God wanted you to be? What was it like? If you haven't, name some practices you could try to experience the joy of being in his presence.

4. James 4:10 instructs us to humble ourselves and wait for God to exalt us. Does this make you feel uncomfortable? Why?

Scripture focus. Memorize 1 Timothy 6:9-10 or 1 Peter 5:6-8. Have you ever asked God not to give you so much that you forget him or to never let you have enough wealth that it is a distraction? Would you be willing to pray a prayer like this? Talk about this with another person.

Practice. Read the paragraph from the text that begins, "Everything is spiritual if the focus of your heart is correct." When you finish, write down all of the practices mentioned to develop more spiritual lives. See if you can name six or seven things you can do to practice. Which of them are commands? Which of them do you practice regularly? Add one of these practices to your daily routine. If you find that you do none of these things right now, you may be discouraged. Don't beat yourself up. You and God are writing a new story. Pick yourself up and start from where you are.

Out of the Woods
and Into the Light

Half way along the road we have to go,
I found myself obscured in a great forest,
Bewildered, and I knew I had lost the way.

Dante Alighieri,
The Divine Comedy, Inferno

—⁓—

In one of the most famous poems of all time,[1] Dante hits
midlife and discovers he's lost. It happens to the best of us.
Sometimes the crisis hits us even earlier along the journey. If we
are sharp enough to force ourselves to slow down and examine
what we've been working toward until now, we may discover that
what looked like treasure is nothing more than emptiness, de-
lusion and foolishness. The things we really wanted most—
fulfillment, reality and wisdom—are nowhere in sight. We are
bewildered, and we know we've lost our way.

Perhaps no one tells the story of being lost like Dante in his
great epic poem *The Divine Comedy*. Written almost seven
hundred years ago, Dante's poem is an autobiographical allegory

of a man's spiritual journey out of a dark wood, up a great mountain and on to paradise. And while Dante's world differed greatly from ours, the fact remains that he was on the same journey through life that many of us are, completely lost in our past as we navigate the present so that we might find an eternal future. Everyone has this longing and is looking for a way out of the forest, but most people don't come into conscious awareness of it until somewhere in the middle of their life's journey or when they encounter a crisis.

When we're faced with a situation that renders us helpless or hopeless, or when we see our capacities diminishing while our responsibilities only seem to be increasing, we find ourselves at an unexpected point of frustration. Suddenly all the things that we had hoped for or had hoped to be able to do are no longer viable options as we come to terms with our own mortality. Many of our fondest aspirations related to family, career, health and even our faith simply haven't happened as we'd hoped. While we knew we were mortal, the momentum we were gaining was beginning to convince us otherwise. So the crisis brings us back to face reality.

Even those few people who *have* achieved enormous amounts of success have found that it's just not enough. The reality check still comes at some point. King Solomon wrote: "Yet when I surveyed all that my hands had done and what I had toiled to achieve, everything was meaningless, a chasing after the wind; nothing was gained under the sun" (Ecclesiastes 2:11). Or as Saint Augustine put it, "You [God] have formed us for Yourself, and our hearts are restless till they find rest in You." However, many times we settle for shortsighted outlets that tickle the senses while depleting the soul. In an odd way, we find ourselves wrestling with our faith while simultaneously ignoring it as we become further distracted by the pleasures of the world.

It's a safe bet to blame it on the world because the system that exists here is completely contrary to the love of God. It will always lead us toward the temporal and reinforce our efforts in that direction. The world won't ever teach us to pursue knowing God over gaining pleasure, approval of God over desiring recognition, servanthood over treasuring popularity, integrity and character over wealth or status, or humility over power. It just can't.

Instead, the world offers us an inevitable progression toward self-centeredness. Need proof? Just look at the progression of magazine titles over the last century: *Time* (1923), *Life* (1936), *People* (1974), *Us Weekly* (1977) and *Self* (1979). Look at people using smartphones as mirrors or the popularity of selfies. I recently heard a group of teen girls talking about the possibility of joining a mission trip. It would be a great place to take selfies with little kids, they said. The world is shouting its shiny but shortsighted directions at us, and they can be overwhelming. It may be difficult to notice the still, small whisper of the Lord while we're busy posting to Instagram.

And so we get lost.

Though some say we shouldn't be so harsh, drawing a false dichotomy between the world's ways and God's—after all, doesn't God love the world? (John 3:16)—we can't say we haven't been warned about a temporal paradigm. We're told in 1 John 2:15-16:

> Do not love the world or anything in the world. If anyone loves the world, love for the Father is not in them. For everything in the world—the lust of the flesh, the lust of the eyes, and the pride of life—comes not from the Father but from the world.

Many people misinterpret this passage and stray toward an old Gnostic belief that matter is the enemy. But God created everything and said that it was good. He made a beautiful world for us, and he gave us dominion over it. The love of the world that John is talking about is something else, as he explains in verse 16. "Everything in the world" that we are being cautioned against are ethical choices, not material possessions. As author Michael Wittmer says in *Heaven Is a Place on Earth*, our problem is "sin, not stuff."[2]

> John's three-fold description of the world—"cravings," "lust," and "boasting" . . . describe sins, not various aspects of reality. The world John is warning us about is not the universe of beautiful things, but the sinful manner in which we often respond to what attracts us (that is, we crave and lust after something and then boast about our accomplishment when we unjustly acquire it).[3]

So, again, the problem is in the paradigm. We must maintain our eternal worldview while living faithfully in this world. But the cravings and lust (and the temptation to boast when we acquire and achieve) seem to pursue us. This is what Dante found. And it is when this temporal, worldly paradigm sneaks in that we must maintain our holy and eternal perspective, just as Dante maintained his focus on the light ahead of him. This world system will perish, but we remind ourselves that "whoever does the will of God lives forever" (1 John 2:17). And we were meant to live forever.

The Leopard and the Lust of the Eyes

In *Inferno*, the first part of Dante's *Divine Comedy*, he is in a daze, having just passed through the shadow lands, and standing at the foot of a majestic hill. Gazing upward, he recognizes the faint outline of the sun behind its peak and begins to climb toward the heavens, relying on his own strength and firm footing.

Within moments, though, he is quickly met by a leopard, a lion and a she-wolf who want to stop him from reaching paradise. Dante sees them for what they are: deterrents. We are not always so clever.

The first beast to oppose him is a leopard that impedes forward movement.

> And, almost at the point where the slope began,
> I saw a leopard, extremely light and active,
> The skin of which was mottled.
>
> And somehow it managed to stay in front of me,
> In such a manner that it blocked my way so much
> That I was often forced to turn back the road I had come. . . .
>
> That wild animal with the brilliant skin.[4]

As our protagonist seeks the brilliance of the light at the top of the hill, he encounters a spotted distraction that was shining with "brilliant skin." Dante is referring to things that cause our focus to drift away from the grandeur of God, creating an obstruction between us and the abundant life we are pursuing in Christ. Often when we see something that excites us, our eyes "light up," and we lose focus. But Jesus warned us against such distractions:

> The eye is the lamp of the body. If your eyes are healthy, your whole body will be full of light. But if your eyes are unhealthy, your whole body will be full of darkness. If then the light within you is darkness, how great is that darkness!
>
> No one can serve two masters. Either you will hate the one and love the other, or you will be devoted to the one and despise the other. You cannot serve both God and money. (Matthew 6:22-24)

Greed. When life is reduced to getting what we do not have and keeping what we do have, we become wrapped in an inordinate desire that creates idolatrous engrossment. Let's be clear here to avoid confusion. Wealth can be very good and can support the work of God's kingdom. But we must be constantly vigilant to avoid relying on God's gifts instead of on God himself.

Whether it is an upgrade on our electronics, a faster car or a bigger house, we must pay close attention to the leopards in our lives. If we're not careful while we are enjoying them, we may lose our focus on our Father. However, if we are divinely mindful we can allow the Lord to use these things as reminders to renew our focus on him.

We have been called to look for the invisible realities that lead us to an everlasting hope. They're around us, but we have to seek them. We're invited to do our seeking in the world in the presence of our neighbors, who (like our enemies) we are called to love with the same measure of grace that we have received. As we extend mercy in a merciless world, we reveal the kingdom of God to those who find it unimaginable.

There is a reason Christians are called "born again." We need to recognize that the resurrection of Jesus Christ offers a real hope that will not deteriorate and a glimpse past the natural order of things. We've been born into something new and become heirs of something imperishable that can't be defiled and won't fade. Mindful of that calling, we gain authority to face this beast and its companions along the way.

THE LION AND THE PRIDE OF AMBITION

As Dante attempts to navigate his way around the leopard through his own power, he suddenly realizes a second beast has come upon the scene:

I found myself without fear
When a lion appeared before me, as it did.

When he came, he made his way towards me
With head high, and seemed ravenously hungry,
So that the air itself was frightened of him.[5]

Ambition is trusting in the wrong thing—ourselves. We tend
to readily place our faith in ourselves and our abilities without
ever recognizing that this will inevitably let us down. The roar
of pride feeds this process by creating the staggered thinking
that we are the supreme objects of trust in the universe. Unfortunately, we learn this is false the hard way as the path we hope
to traverse leads us into a territory of predators. Often the very
good things that we long to say, think and do elude us in practice
as the daily urge of ambition prowls around, seeking to devour
any desire we have to serve the Lord.

In the midst of this most serious distraction, we get lost when
we forget how to hope. We can hope *for* things in the world. But
we hope *in* the eternal. We might hope *for* something material
such as a better job or lifestyle. We can hope for all kinds of
things, and there's nothing wrong with that. The problem comes
when ambition leads us to hope *in* them because they are not
strong enough to bear the weight of that kind of hope. There's
only one that strong, and that's Jesus Christ. So the wise choice
is to put our hope in him and hold our temporal hopes with a
loose grip so that it doesn't destroy us if they are not realized.
The crisis instead becomes a process as we recognize that we
won't achieve a certain goal or watch a dream go unfulfilled. In
the midst of mourning the loss of these things, we realize that
we're okay as long as our Father is with us.

Even if we have come to the intellectual conclusion that Jesus
is Savior, it takes tremendous energy and continual commitment

to order our daily lives around the core conviction that he is Lord and we are not. This is where the rubber meets the road. But keeping the rubber to the road is precisely how we show we are serious about our commitment to him. We daily recommit our lives to him, telling him our hopes and dreams but also being open to his plans for us and capitulating to his will. We find—without fail—that his plans are always much better than ours were anyway.

Some serious risk is going to be involved if we're going to stay committed. But faith always requires risk. Christianity isn't just a question of knowing truth, it's also a matter of completely consigning our lives to a God we know to be good and who has the best intentions for us. If we genuinely hope to rethink our daily urges, we must embrace the *content* of Scripture within the *context* of our lives. And we *must* learn to trust. It's the only way.

When I was thirteen years old, I came to an intellectual belief that Jesus was who he claimed to be. That seemed to be enough at the time, and so for another eight years I lived under the impression that I largely understood what Christianity was about. Deep in my heart, though, I knew better and began to realize that something was awry. But I didn't want to deal with it directly because I was comfortable believing the decision I'd made earlier was enough in the grand scheme of things.

It wasn't until I was nineteen that I realized I didn't have any true answers to the questions of life, and it wasn't until I was twenty-one that I felt compelled to get off the fence I had been sitting on. In retrospect, I can now see that God had been manifesting himself in powerful ways all along and authoring a question within me about how I was really going to live my life. When this all became clear, it was as if the decision had been made for me. This turning point from intellectual assent to personal reception made all the difference for me.

You see, Christianity is trust in a person—not belief in a proposition. This doesn't dismiss the idea of propositional truth in any way; God's Word is filled with it, and it's important. But the propositions of Christianity are simply not enough. None of us can *do* what Christ calls us to do if we don't have the strength and the courage that comes from a relationship with him. We must move beyond propositions and into relationship with the person to whom the truths all point and describe. We're called to pursue and trust in Jesus alone.

When we seek first the Lion of Judah (a name for God that goes back all the way to the book of Genesis) and *his* righteousness, we become more able to pursue our temporal hopes with a loose grip. Then the hunt doesn't destroy us. The secular and the sacred inform each other in this way, creating an amalgamated perspective that causes us to search for a greater life than we would have otherwise pursued. Likewise, the union of the two perspectives offers a valuable insight into the value of excellence as we "serve wholeheartedly, as if [we] were serving the Lord, not people" (Ephesians 6:7).

While it is natural to hope for a healthy measure of power and goods in the temporal, we must allow the Holy Spirit to hold us accountable for our motives. We must consider whether the goal is to be able to boast about our success or to gain a position that will empower us to do greater things for the Lord. If our goal is to be pleasing to the Lord, we can maintain a poverty of spirit within while avoiding a dangerous pitfall. Os Guinness explained that pride is

the first, worst, and most prevalent of the seven deadly sins. It is either the source or the chief component of all other sin. . . . Its source is neither the world nor the flesh, but the Devil. . . . The modern world has transformed this vice into a virtue [by confusing it with self-respect].[6]

Perhaps the chief thing wrong with pride is that it puts the love of self above the love of God. When self-love is placed above the love of God, it becomes idolatry but when love of God is given the highest priority, love leads to sanctification. Throughout *The Divine Comedy*, we find Christ as a character in both the foreground and the background. His grace allows Dante's ambition to drive the protagonist upward, even if it does require a journey through purgatory. While we may not agree entirely with Dante's theology, we can greatly appreciate his imagery. He clearly shows the sanctification process as one in which God reveals what is sin so that we can respond to his convicting grace. Frankly, that's what life is about once you come into the kingdom of God through a relationship with Christ. The sanctification process—the process of setting our lives apart for him—with its purgation, begins taking place.

Unfortunately, ambition can sidetrack us, leave us in despair and lead us away from those who might set us back on track. C. S. Lewis said:

> It is pride which has been the chief cause of misery in every nation and every family since the world began. Other vices may sometimes bring people together: you may find good fellowship and jokes and friendliness among drunken people or unchaste people. But Pride . . . is enmity.[7]

We must recognize this in order to avoid falling prey to this ravenous brute.

The lion precedes one last beast that attempts to drive Dante back down into the darkness of the valley.

THE SHE-WOLF AND THE LUST OF THE FLESH

Dante finds himself exasperated through the recounting of his third attacker:

And a she-wolf, who seemed, in her thinness,
To have nothing but excessive appetites,
And she has already made many miserable.

She weighed down so heavily upon me
With that fear, which issued from her image,
That I lost hope of reaching the top of the hill.

And, like a man whose mind is on his winnings,
When the time comes for him to lose,
And all his thoughts turn into sorrow and tears:

So I was transformed by that restless animal
Who came against me, and gradually drove me down,
Back to the region where the sun is silent.[8]

It takes only a glance at our calendar or checkbook to see what the excessive appetites and highest priorities are in our lives. How we spend our time, talents and treasures is revealed when we allow the lust of our flesh to weigh down heavily upon us. The world and the objects of the appetites it loves to feed are constantly in our view. And we can literally be transformed by it as our focus shifts and we turn our backs, if at first only slightly, on God. Then we're once again headed into the darkness.

Jesus explained that fleshly lust dehumanizes people in our minds before it dehumanizes them in physical action. While some would find it appalling to consider slavery a healthy ideal in today's society, most would never make the connection that creating a fantasy life involving another person is the mental and spiritual equivalent. Social critic Henry Fairlie differentiates between the she-wolf and the true love she was counterfeited after:

Lust dies at the next dawn, and when it returns in the evening, to search where it may, it is with its own past erased. Love wants to enjoy in other ways the human being whom it has enjoyed in bed; it looks forward to having breakfast. But in the morning Lust is always furtive. It dresses as mechanically as it undressed and heads straight for the door, to return to its own solitude.[9]

As Dante faces the restlessness of the she-wolf, he finds himself lacking the imagination and opportunity to conceive of a way of getting past her. Her presence and her image steal, kill and destroy any hope he has of reaching the heavens he had aspired to, and he is forced back down the mountain and in need of divine aid.

CRYING OUT FOR HELP!

To avoid being destroyed by the beasts, Dante cries out for help. We know this pattern all too well. Sadly, it often seems as though things have to come to the end of the road before we cry out for assistance. I sometimes wonder what God thinks about being our last refuge instead of our first proponent. Frankly, I don't know how he puts up with us. We don't usually come to him out of pure motives. Perhaps this is why he sometimes removes things from our lives that we hold dear—to turn our focus back to him and to remind us where our attention belongs.

In Dante's allegory, his prayer is answered through the ghost of the Latin poet Virgil, an author who died more than a thousand years earlier and served as a distant influence on Dante. Virgil becomes a guide through the dark forest into the depths of hell and finally toward a new ascent. Dante soon realizes that Virgil can only carry him so far and cannot enter the ultimate realm of paradise because he is still a pagan with worldly wisdom and insight. As the two navigate toward heaven the hard way, they witness the sufferings of those people who fully abandoned themselves to the beasts to be devoured.

Throughout our own journey in life, we are called to pay attention to the anguish of others so that we might better understand the reality of eternity in the process (Jude 7). This sifting of sin around us can create a redemptive experience within us that God uses to reveal where we are in our own process. This examination is necessary in that one day we must all appear before the divine judgment seat of Christ and give an account ourselves. Each person's work will be tested through fire, allowing whatever remains to become a reward while everything else burned off. The gold, silver and precious things that remain are there because we have asked the tough questions and fixed our eyes on Christ.

In Dante's work, we find Christ entering heaven through various crystalline spheres, each one higher than the other. The poem ends by focusing on the great image of three circles of light that are not each other but yet are one.

When we find ourselves in crisis, our pain and frustration will lead us to look for answers. But in the end, we find ourselves coming to terms with ambiguity, knowing that we don't, and may never, have all the answers. Amazingly, we can trust the one who does and who has already been through everything we are facing. We can quit trying to control the uncontrollable and acquire the unobtainable. Some of us may learn only because of a crisis that the hope of heaven is alive though Jesus Christ.

Every human being who loses his or her way has usually bought into the world's promises. But Jesus, who went through the greatest inferno of all, can help us to rethink our daily struggles and find eternal hope in the middle of any crisis. We can discover the kingdom of heaven on earth—something so indescribable and beyond the realm of human imagination that no human poet would ever have the artistic resources to capture it.

FOR FURTHER REFLECTION

1. Name the three beasts Dante faced on his journey in *The Divine Comedy*. What do they represent?

2. Read Matthew 4 or Luke 4 about the temptation of Jesus in the wilderness. Identify which temptation represents each of Dante's three beasts. What was Jesus' response to each?

3. Read the quote from Os Guinness in the chapter. Do you agree or disagree with what he says about pride? Why? Discuss with another person.

4. How does C. S. Lewis say pride is different from other sins?

Scripture focus. Memorize 1 John 2:15-16.

Practice. Consider giving up television, movies, social media or games on your smartphone for a week. Commit to using the device you carry with you daily only as an old-school telephone would be used. Can you do it? Do these things hold too tight a grip on your life? Do you rationalize that you need them when maybe you really don't?

What Do You Seek?
(Your Heart's Intention)

—៣—

There is an old story of an enormous Navy cargo ship that was making its way to a port in South Carolina one night. When a blip appeared on the ship's radar screen, the captain said to his radio operator, "Order that ship to alter its course fifteen degrees." The message was sent. A response came that surprised the captain: "*You* change *your* course fifteen degrees!" Knowing he had the right of way, the captain repeated his instructions: "Tell that ship it must alter its course fifteen degrees!" The response was again: "*You* must change *your* course fifteen degrees!" The captain grabbed the handset from the radio operator and barked into it himself: "I am the captain of a US Navy cargo ship. I have the right of way, and I order you to change your course fifteen degrees!" The voice on the other side responded: "Captain, I am a lighthouse; I cannot alter my course!"

Even on our best days, we all make assumptions. With hindsight, we see that some of them were very foolish. Some were based on ideas about our own importance. Many weren't thought out very well. Others were presuppositions we weren't even aware we held. As A. W. Tozer said, "The history of mankind will probably show that no people has ever risen above its religion, and man's spiritual history will positively demonstrate that no religion has ever been greater than its idea of God."[1]

We have our own ideas about who God is and who we are in relation to him, but regardless of whether we are aware of them or whether we've thought them through to their logical conclusions, our presuppositions *will* shape our perspective and eventually our actions. Having set ourselves in the context of God's story, it behooves us to examine the things to which we claim to be committed, and the things to which we actually *are* committed. Problems will arise when we don't think through these things carefully, when we aren't even aware what it is we are actually seeking.

So, what do you seek? It's the first question Jesus is recorded as having asked in the gospels.

> The next day again John was standing with two of his disciples; and he looked at Jesus as he walked, and said, "Behold, the Lamb of God!" The two disciples heard him say this, and they followed Jesus. Jesus turned, and saw them following, and said to them, "What do you seek?" And they said to him, "Rabbi" (which means Teacher), "where are you staying?" He said to them, "Come and see." They came and saw where he was staying; and they stayed with him that day. (John 1:35-39 RSV)

These clear-cut but thought-provoking verses really show that the intention of your heart is the most important thing about you. *What do you wish; what do you seek?* There are a million reasons people come to Jesus. In this instance, Jesus doesn't want to know *why* they are coming to him; he wants to know *what they want from him*! Do *you* know what you want from Jesus? Compassion? Healing? Direction? Or maybe you, like the disciples, are more concerned with simply spending the day with him. He is here. He is not silent, and not only will he reveal himself to you in surprising ways, but he also may just reveal your own intention for finding him in the first place. You just have to ask.

Clearly we don't often recognize our own motivations. And often we fail to stick to an eternal paradigm precisely because we haven't examined the nonnegotiable things to which we claim to be committed. We haven't thought them through to their logical conclusions. As Christians, there are some primary beliefs that we must not let go. Theologian Francis Schaeffer described the most important of these, the bedrock presupposition for all Christians, in his book of the same name: *He Is There and He Is Not Silent.*

God Is Here; He Is Not Silent

The author of all creation has revealed himself to humanity "at many times and in various ways" (Hebrews 1:1) through creation, in our consciences, by dreams, visions, prophets and apostles, and most decisively in the person and work of Jesus Christ. The clearest and highest form of personal revelation is God coming down and becoming one of us. The story of Jesus is not that a man became God but that God became one of us. Because he did this, he understands what it's like to be tempted, to suffer rejection, hardship, fatigue, hunger, thirst, betrayal and all the other things that we suffer. As Scripture says, we have a high priest who can sympathize with all of our weakness (Hebrews 4:15). No matter where you are or what you are going through, Jesus can relate.

He became one of us so that he can lift us up into the glory of his own life. God's incarnate revelation (Christ, himself, in the flesh) is the clearest declaration of who God is. If you want to know the Father, look at the Son. If you want to see how the Father loves you, look at how the Son loved those who surrounded and followed him. If you want to know how the Father suffers for you, look at how the Son suffered for you.

We often think that God the Father is impassable and doesn't have any feelings, but this isn't true. Jesus had a rich emotional life, and he is the perfect image of who God is. It grieves God when we do not live our lives to the fullest of our calling. Though he doesn't need us, he chooses to make his joy related to ours. We don't understand why, but Scripture attests to the truth of it.

The Bible is God's declaration of his character and ways, his love letter to the people he sent his Son to redeem and his blueprint for how to live life. Scripture is what we use to renew our mind, develop a Christlike pattern of thinking and grow close to God. To do this, we have to develop habits of engaging with Scripture.

The Bible can teach us how to live life with wisdom, purpose, faith, hope and love. And God knows we want these things. But we will never get these great things by seeking *them*. We will never find those things as ends in themselves. We will only find them as the byproduct of the pursuit of God. They are the overflow of pursuing him above everything else.

Scripture says, "Seek first his kingdom and his righteousness, and all these things will be given to you as well" (Matthew 6:33). When nothing is given to us, we probably left out the word "first" in the intention of our hearts. Seek *first*, not second or third. If you pursue second things above first things, you won't attain them. And you'll miss the first things as well. Pursue the gifts instead of the giver, and you'll get neither. Pursue the giver, and all you need will come from the overflow of your relationship with him.

WE *BELIEVE* IT; DO WE *MEAN* IT?

Imagine a scene in which a five-year-old girl appears in her father's office dressed all in pale turquoise blue with a crown on her head and a wand in her hand. "Ta-daaa!" she says. "I'm Queen Elsa, and you are frozen!" The father snickers but goes back to his paperwork. She taps his back and waves her hand to freeze him and says again, "I'm Elsa!" So he pretends to be stuck and struggling against the freezing cold . . . for about twenty seconds. The little girl whines, "Aw, Daaaaad! You have to at least *act* like you believe it!"

Isn't that our problem too? Frequently, we're just playing. We're not *acting* like we believe.

But if I trust that my story is a part of the Lord's, then I better know his story and act on my belief in it. If my fundamental belief is that God is here and he is not silent, everything I *do* should flow from these beliefs. I should not only acknowledge his presence but also learn to *listen* to him. The core concepts that God is and that he speaks should shape my perspective on everything. Who is God? Who am I? Where did we come from? Why are we here? Where are we going, and how should we relate to each other?

Astrobiologist and cosmologist Carl Sagan said on PBS's *Cosmos*, "The cosmos is all that ever was, is, or ever will be." That's a faith proposition. No scientific observation can tell you that. The limits of science are very profound, so claiming that science has all the answers is a statement of faith. Cosmology is a volatile science. If you work in this field, your job is to determine how the universe began. And I can promise you, the theory of today will not be the same as what is popular years from now. If a cosmologist marries himself to the theory of today, he'll be a widower in a few years. And yet people still hold these things as if they're absolutely proven and absolutely true.

Why? Because people don't want to live by faith. They want to have some sense of authority, and they think science gives it to them. Unfortunately, you and I can be that way as well. But if we choose well, our authority will come from God's revealed Word. We have bedrock, a final authority, and our assumptions have profound implications.

Here's the point: everybody has a faith system, even atheist scientists. If you press a person hard enough there are, deep down, at least some nebulous ideas about the answers to those questions that a worldview answers. Unfortunately, most people have left their presuppositions in this nebulous state, and that is not a very strong foundation on which to build a life. Few people can articulate their own belief system, and of the small number of people who *can* articulate their worldview, an even smaller percentage of people have thought through the logical implications of how their worldview would require them to live. And *then*, of this tiny percentage, only a handful of people have actually followed these implications to their logical conclusions.

What about you? Can you articulate what you believe? More to the point, does your behavior align with what you say you believe? As we have seen, we all have a worldview that shapes our understanding of our identity, origin and destiny and how we ought to live in this world. In other words, our worldview informs our values, and those values influence our behavior. And here is why that matters: your behavior is what the world sees.

If God is here, and he is not silent—if God is a Trinity of being, a community who is personal and has created us in his image for relationship with him, if he has really revealed himself in various, diverse ways—then that has implications. God is either a very big deal or no deal at all, but he cannot be moderately important. Unfortunately, moderately important is exactly how many of us seem to view him.

The present and active communication from God gives Christians the very foundations for living, and our lives must attest to our understanding that God as ultimate reality determines how we should live.

A TALE OF TWO CHOICES?

> *It was the best of times. It was the worst of the times.*
> *It was the age of wisdom. It was the age of foolishness.*
> *It was the epic of belief. It was the epic of incredulity.*
> *It was the season of light. It was the season of darkness.*
> *It was the spring of hope. It was the winter of despair.*
>
> CHARLES DICKENS

In what is perhaps the most famous precursory statement in literature, in *A Tale of Two Cities* Dickens accurately describes many eras that pass.[2] It is as true now as it was then. It is fair to say that we now live simultaneously in an age of belief and an age of incredulity. People have never been more gullible than they are now, and there has never been such skepticism.

And in this age in which we now live, many people have largely surrendered the right to think. Questions such as "What do we believe?" and "What is our role?" and "What should we do?" frequently don't get asked. If Christians begin examining their paradigms, there will be more answers to these questions. If we examine our basic, fundamental beliefs about who God is, we will work our way down through the rest of our beliefs and follow this belief system to the ultimate question: what do you seek? We will be able to answer it intelligibly—and ask it of others with conviction.

Always be prepared to give an answer to everyone who
asks you to give the reason for the hope that you have.
(1 Peter 3:15)

We must first establish who we believe God is. Then we can
begin to think about who we are in light of having been created
in his image. This can be followed by thinking through who
God is and to what he calls us. How should I think in light of
this? How should I live? But we must always start with the top
down, letting our answer to the question "Who is God?"
inform our answer to the questions "Who am I?" and "How
shall I live my life?"

So, what comes into your mind when *you* think about God?
Tozer says we might predict with certainty the spiritual future of
each man if we knew that answer because what we think about
God is the most important thing about us.[3]

Years ago a young musician named Phil befriended a homeless
guy near the youth camp he was attending. So he invited this
fellow right into the camp, let him hang around the kids and
even invited him to eat dinner at his table. At first the kids were
wary of this man, but with time they all found they enjoyed his
company and came to accept him. Maybe he didn't have money
in his pocket, but there was profound wisdom in his words.
When they were all waiting for the guest speaker to take the
podium that evening, they noticed this man get up from his
chair, walk down the aisle and begin to remove his tattered
jacket. He wiped the make-up "dirt" from his face, and there
stood their guest speaker sporting a T-shirt that read, "Who Do
You Say I Am?"

Phil immediately realized the point the guest speaker was
trying to make by dressing up as a homeless man. That night, he
went into his cabin and wrote these words:

Who do you say I am?
Do you know of my life or have you ever heard of me?

Who do you say I am?
Won't you take the time to know me?

I am Jesus Christ the Lamb.[4]

Sometimes God is like this guest speaker; he reveals himself to us in ways we weren't expecting. And it brings us back to the question of worldview—*the first question about who we are is about who we say God is.* With that in mind, and remembering the basic presuppositions that God exists and decisively revealed himself in Christ and the Scriptures, what are the logical implications? There may be many, but if we look at Colossians 1:15-20, we have to say that the most important is that *life is all about God and not about us.* All things have been created by him and for him, and we exist to serve God, not to try to persuade God to serve us. If we apply this, it might very well change how many of us pray.

In essence, the Bible reminds us again and again that he is God and we are not. And we have a choice to make—wisdom or foolishness? Belief or incredulity? Light or darkness? Hope or despair? We must recognize the world system for what it is with these opposing extremes of belief, and we must not fall to either side. It may sound like a tale of two choices, but it is really more about knowing the answer concerning what we think about God before we can ever truly make any choice at all. Pastor Louie Giglio said:

> There's a Story that has been going on long before you arrived on planet earth and one that will go on long after you're gone.
>
> God is the central character of this preemptive and prevailing Story, and He is the central character of this book.

He commands center stage in existence, creation, time, life, history, redemption, and eternity. . . .

I'm not trying to put you down or imply that you don't matter. Nor am I saying that you are absent from the grand Story of God. In fact, just the opposite. Amazingly, you appear on every page, existing in God's thoughts long before this world was made. I'm simply stating the obvious—that the story already has a star, and the star is not you or me. [5]

And here's why that matters: if we don't get the story straight, everything else in our lives will be out of sync.

In Sync

"I am God, and you're not." We might forget that when we make ourselves into our own little gods, tiny autonomous agents who suppose we can control and create. But as Christians, we must constantly come to terms with the reality of that proposition: *God is God, and I am not.* And when we discover that our lives are centered on him, we'll find our lives given back to us.

Whoever finds their life will lose it, and whoever loses their life for my sake will find it. (Matthew 10:39)

It's not that God's some divine tyrant saying, "You do this, or else here's the consequence." Rather, we do what he asks because he is the source of all beauty, truth and goodness. It would be spiritual, moral and intellectual insanity to ignore or even fight against this source. It is right and proper for us to maintain the perspective that God is God, and life is about him. In his service is our perfect freedom. And we are free only when we serve Christ. We are slaves when we serve any other master. Though it may be a little difficult to comprehend, that really is what it comes down to in our understanding of the world.

> For us there is but one God, the Father, from whom all things came and for whom we live; and there is but one Lord, Jesus Christ, through whom all things came and through whom we live. (1 Corinthians 8:6)

We exist for him and not for ourselves. This is one reason Jesus had to ask the question (and he asks us over and over) in the first chapter of John: *What do you seek?* But remember the answer? It wasn't about theology or philosophy or grasping all the answers of the world through him in that one moment. The answer was in his reply, "Come, and you will see." *And they went and spent the day with him.*

What are the logical implications of the view that the infinite and personal God exists, has decisively revealed himself in Christ and the Scriptures and wants a relationship with us? Let us sum them up.

- Since we were created for relationship with the Author of every good thing, our purpose is to know him and become like him.

- Since the Bible was inspired by God, we need to learn, understand, experience and apply its precepts and principles.

- Scripture is countercultural, so while we are on this earth, we will always experience a tension; we will seek to live our lives one way and constantly be pulled toward another.

Life with Jesus is a gift, but it seems that when we get a great gift, we go immediately for it instead of toward the giver, and then we forget the giver altogether . . . at least for a time. But God knows our weaknesses (Hebrews 4:15). He doesn't wait until we have perfect motives in pursuing him. If he did, nobody would ever make it. But at least we can work toward his finding pleasure in our efforts.

The standard is Christ himself. God is God, and I am not, and it would be great if our joy was actually made perfect in *embracing that*!

> For in him all things were created: things in heaven and on earth, visible and invisible, whether thrones or powers or rulers or authorities; all things have been created through him and for him. He is before all things, and in him all things hold together. (Colossians 1:16-17)

We look to him for himself, and our joy is the byproduct of the course we choose.

ALTER YOUR COURSE

I don't want to minimize the importance of grasping your resources in Christ as you struggle against the temporal system. You have the resource of the power of the Holy Spirit if you invite him to reign in your life and keep re-inviting him to do that whenever you try to take back control. And if you'll also use Scripture to renew your mind with an eternal perspective, you'll see temporal things in a different light.

All along we've been asking the question, "How then shall we live?" Phil's guest speaker asked a similar question, "Who do you say I am?" And these questions hold the same delivery value as Jesus' first question to his disciples, "What do you seek?" So ensues the quest: if you are a follower of Christ, you must find the real you and the *intention of your heart*. Who is the deepest you? Who is Christ in you? Do you have the hope of glory; is it manifest through you? This is the real longing and intention of your heart.

There are flaws in everyone's understanding of God. No one understands him perfectly, apart from Jesus. But if the intention of your heart is to be in relationship with Jesus, your broken story will be better than pieced back together. Your course will be altered; your ship will sail safe waters, and no lighthouse will have to force you to adjust your route. Instead it will be altered by knowing who he is. He will not have to disguise himself in order to ask, "Who do you say I am?" You will already know God and believe, and then you'll know how to live because you have found him at the very core of your worldview.

FOR FURTHER REFLECTION

1. Read the paragraph from the text that begins, "All along we've been asking the question. . . ." Define the intention of your heart.

2. How does God communicate with you? If your answer is that you don't feel much like he does, pray and ask that he will begin to communicate with you in a way that you can sense and understand.

Scripture focus. Begin to memorize Colossians 1:15-20. Is this how you thought of Jesus before you began committing this to memory?

Practice. Answer these questions with answers that state your worldview and discuss them with a spiritual mentor. After you've written out your worldview, look at each category and ask yourself, "Does my behavior match up with what I say I believe?"

- Who is God?
- Who am I?
- Where did we all come from?
- Why are we here?
- Where are we going?
- How should we relate to each other?

Further practice. It matters what we seek. What are you seeking? Do an Internet search or ask a spiritual mentor about ways God's people have sought him historically and practice one of them.

Becoming a
Permanent Marker

—ɯ—

I came across this little poem a few years ago.

When as a child I laughed and wept,
Time crept.
When as a youth I waxed more bold,
Time *strolled*.
When I became a full grown man,
Time RAN.
When older still I daily grew,
Time **FLEW**.
Soon shall I find, in passing on,
Time *gone*.

Time creeps, then it walks. It runs. It flies, and then it's gone.[1] That's profound and pithy, but it's pessimistic, and no matter what your story, it could cause you to lose hope. Either time is dragging along or it seems to be slipping away from us.

Instead, let's look at life from the perspective of those who presuppose that God is present and not silent regarding the details and direction of our lives. Time still passes, but for those of us who hold such a perspective, there is a better understanding of how even the smallest daily decisions find their own place in the mosaic of eternity. Time moves on, but it's never *gone*. It's invested. Every action matters; every day is an opportunity to make preparation for eternity a priority. And together we all play a part in a story that is much bigger than any one of us and more wonderful than we could ever imagine.

A person who cannot see past secular goals of achievement will never fully realize how his compartmentalization has made the largest thing in life his own ego. But if life is truly the story of God and our finding our own role in that story, then this shortsightedness has idolatrous implications that shouldn't be ignored.

Either now or some day sooner than we expect, time will seem to be gaining on us regardless of our perspective or worldview. In light of that fact, it would be wise for us to ask ourselves some serious questions: "How do I want to make my mark on this world?" and "Is what I'm working toward now something that will last forever?" and "Whom do I serve?"

An eternal perspective will always lead us to make preparation for eternity a priority. But it is easy to get off track. You may want to take a break from reading to think about and maybe even write down your answers to these questions.

Making a Mark

I once accidentally picked up a Sharpie permanent marker to write on the whiteboard during a class I was teaching. Needless to say, no matter what kind of scrubbing I did to get that stuff off, it was on that board forever. But isn't that really the kind of permanence we all want to achieve in life, not on our whiteboards? We don't want to be forgotten. And so those of us with an eternal perspective hope and believe that the decisions we make and actions we take can contribute to a larger story—not the story of us that will go down in history but the story of God, the permanent marker version, that will go on into eternity. Choosing an eternal paradigm means choosing to live a life that matters forever rather than a life that makes a mark now but is easily erased in the long run.

I remember feeling uncomfortable some years ago when a friend said to me, "I want to make a difference in the world. I don't care how I do it; I just want people to remember me after I die."

My friend is not alone in wanting to pursue things that she thinks the world will declare to be important. We all want to do something that will matter forever. But (though she does not know it) this is no way to leave a *permanent* mark. You can't make a permanent mark with a crayon. We serve a God who measures by the intention of our hearts, and *how* we do what we do *does* matter for eternity no matter how long our name is remembered. And it matters even more whether we are trying to please God or win the admiration of people.

We all want to matter and know that we are significant. We want to be sure that we haven't wasted the lives we've been given. We don't want our names to disappear from people's minds as the eraser of time travels on across that whiteboard. However, an eternal perspective will lead us away from the world's methods for making an impact and toward seeing our time here as an investment in eternity.

How Jesus Made a Mark

In the movie *City Slickers*, Billy Crystal plays Mitch Robbins, a bored baby boomer who sells radio advertising time. One day, he visits his son's school on Career Day. In one of this film's greatest moments, he strays from his speech about his vocation and begins to tell a room full of bewildered students:

Value this time in your life, kids, because this is the time in
your life when you still have your choices, and it goes by so
fast. When you're a teenager you think you can do anything, and you do. Your twenties are a blur. Your thirties,
you raise your family, you make a little money and you
think to yourself, "What happened to my twenties?" Your
forties, you grow a little pot belly, you grow another chin.
The music starts to get too loud. One of your old girlfriends
from high school becomes a grandmother. Your fifties you
have a minor surgery. You'll call it a "procedure," but it's a
surgery. Your sixties you have a major surgery; the music
is still loud, but it doesn't matter because you can't hear it
anyway. Seventies, you and the wife retire to Fort Lau-
derdale; you start eating dinner at two, lunch around ten,
breakfast the night before. And you spend most of your
time wandering around malls looking for the ultimate in
soft yogurt and muttering, "How come the kids don't call?"
By your eighties, you've had a major stroke, and you end up
babbling to some Jamaican nurse who your wife can't stand
but who you call mama. Any questions?[2]

The camera cuts to the kids, who have blank stares of incom-
prehension. They have *no idea* what they have just encoun-
tered. But the movie audience knows that they have just seen
a man who is certain that what he is doing doesn't matter. To
Robbins, life is vaporous, and it is evident by his amusing
oration that he is thrashing about desperately to find his own
significance. While this speech makes us all laugh, it illustrates
well the blur that life can become and the desperate desire we
all have for meaning.

What might Robbins have done to give his life more meaning?
What are we doing now toward that end? As usual, when we look

to Jesus as our model, he turns everything upside down. Jesus Christ, the best-known name ever to walk this earth, made his mark by giving everything for his *Father's* glory (rather than his own) and for *our* benefit (rather than his own).

Serving someone else isn't usually our first thought. We labor to make a mark and woo the world. But Jesus bore our marks in order to save the world. What a difference! When he hung on the cross and proclaimed, "It is finished," he was speaking of a completed work. All sins past, present and future have been paid in full for anyone who will receive him as Lord and Savior. Jesus made his mark by descending to you and me—just as we are— and he was elevated only by the will of his Father. Our goal should be to attain the same kind of mind-set Jesus had.

> Who, being in very nature God,
>   did not consider equality with God something to be
>   used to his own advantage;
> rather, he made himself nothing
>   by taking the very nature of a servant,
>   being made in human likeness.
> And being found in appearance as a man,
>   he humbled himself
>   by becoming obedient to death—
>   even death on a cross!
>
> Therefore God exalted him to the highest place
>   and gave him the name that is above every name,
> that at the name of Jesus every knee should bow,
>   in heaven and on earth and under the earth,
> and every tongue acknowledge that Jesus Christ is Lord,
>   to the glory of God the Father. (Philippians 2:6-11)

Wow! The most permanent mark ever made on this world was accomplished by one who descended, served, poured himself out and humbled himself. As a result of his descent, our hearts can now ascend in response to the overtures of a God who loves us, chases us and draws us to himself. One we may have understood to be a distant tyrant is no such thing. Instead, he pursues us and calls us beloved friends and children. And it was the choice of one man, God's Son, to serve his Father so that we could learn to serve him too.

We live in a broken world, and it's very difficult for us to see that serving God could be a way to make our own names last forever. We are tempted to seek God on our own terms and by our own merits, not by humbling ourselves. The divine longing to reconnect with our Creator causes us to aspire to something that exceeds our own abilities. Many of us long for the greater thing but settle for the lesser thing that has the appearance of the divine, never involving the enabling grace of the Messiah.

THE MARK OF TRUST

As in many world languages, Greek has two words for "knowing," and understanding them both can help us see this issue in a practical sense. The word οἶδα (*oida*) refers to intellectual or cognitive knowledge, while γινώσκω (*ginōskō*) deals with experiential or personal knowledge. Many of the apostle Paul's prayers for the church refer to the latter definition, citing that a genuine comprehension of the Lord comes through real acts of faith. It's the difference between having an academic knowledge of how a parachute works and actually strapping the thing on and jumping out of an airplane. Only one of these will allow us to *experience* the reality.

Making a permanent mark in the world requires a radical perspective—an attitude of dependence upon God, trusting in him like we trust in that parachute. If the first presupposition of Christianity is that God exists, and his Spirit guides us to the story of the Father through the incarnation of the Son, then this second presupposition must follow: there can be no higher purpose than to grow in our relationship and trust of him. This is an investment that is guaranteed to provide dividends in eternity. This experiential learning allows us to know him less by hearsay and more by acquaintance as we seek to conform our hearts and minds to his and become increasingly more like him.

TIME, CHANCE AND PRESUMPTION

Even though we are all eternal beings, there is no way of avoiding the dimension of time. We must use the moments we've been given on this side of eternity to invite Christ into our hearts, allowing him to adjust our core intentions as we weave our lives into the fabric of his story. This way, every facet of our lives can become spiritual through God's divine grace when they are set apart for him. Nothing else matters if it's not somehow related to him and his transcendent kingdom. He is God, and we are not; all of life is about him, not us. The implications of this are nothing short of astounding, and the only mark that matters is the one that he asks us to make.

In 1993, actor and martial artist Brandon Bruce Lee (son of famous martial artist Bruce Lee) died at the age of twenty-eight after a shooting accident on the set of his film *The Crow*. When he died, Lee left behind his fiancée, two multi-picture movie deals and what appeared to be many years of success in career and life ahead of him. Lee's wedding was scheduled to take place just seventeen days after his death, and on the wedding invitation he had quoted a passage from Paul Bowles's book *The Sheltering Sky*. The words are weighty and prophetic:

> Because we do not know when we will die, we get to think
> of life as an inexhaustible well. And yet everything happens

only a certain number of times and a very small number, really. How many more times will you remember a certain afternoon of your childhood, an afternoon that is so deeply a part of your being that you can't even conceive of your life without it? Perhaps four or five times more? Perhaps not even that. How many more times will you watch the full moon rise? Perhaps twenty. And yet it all seems limitless.[3]

Lee never knew how prescient those words were. He never did see another full moon rise. But that is the wisdom of not being presumptuous. There's a tremendous danger in presuming upon the future, especially when it leads to the belief that you have all the time in the world. This is the mistake many of us make and a reason why the unexpected funerals of those whom we care about can catch us off guard.

Unlike Lee, a lot of people *are* presumptuous about the time they've been granted. Some have considered a shift to an eternal paradigm but found the temporal more appealing and assumed that they could deal with the issue of God later. They may have never articulated this belief out loud, yet deep down they are thinking it, "Church, God—yeah, that'll have to wait." They get married, have kids and maybe start thinking about it again, but it's understandable that a decision about God most often turns out to be permanent indecision when put off. If we have spent the entire journey of our lives avoiding God, why would we imagine an authentic change of heart would come later on?

If we live a long life, it is more likely that our final days on this earth will reflect a culmination of our earlier days, especially when it comes to habits and perspectives. Making the most of time means we begin to examine these perspectives now. How do we intend to make our mark? Whom will we choose to serve? Will what we are pursuing now really matter forever?

REDEEMING THE TIME AND KEEPING OUR PROMISE

Teach us to number our days,
that we may gain a heart of wisdom.

PSALM 90:12

In Scripture, a covenant was a binding relationship between a superior party and lesser party. This action symbolized each individual's willingness to give his own life to keep the agreement. To break a covenant was to invite one's own death as penalty.

During the last supper before his crucifixion, Jesus proclaimed, "This is my blood of the covenant, which is poured out for many for the forgiveness of sins" (Matthew 26:28). This statement refers to an extraordinarily unique picture of God as the one who makes the covenant, keeps the covenant and empowers us to honor the covenant. We would do well to take the Scriptures as more than a contract or historical document but instead as an active love letter from the Lord. The same God who made a covenant with Abraham to create a great nation of people makes a covenant with us through Jesus Christ. Our God makes his mark by descending to us. Author Mont Smith puts it this way:

> In the very act of approaching Abraham with a covenant, God was offering to seriously limit His power. For when one makes a promise, he has eliminated a great many possible future actions. He must do that one act. God was committed to a whole series of actions as a result of the covenant with Abraham.[4]

And he is committed to keeping his covenant made through his Son with us. Think about that for a minute. This is an awesome revelation. And it should shed some light on all of the other covenant relationships we have as well. We can begin to view all human promises and agreements as something more than what they seem on the surface. When a man and a woman enter into marriage, they are not just covenanting with each other, they are covenanting with God as the two become one flesh. Likewise, when we serve a human authority, we can actually work with wholehearted integrity keeping our covenant with God and with our earthly masters by working for the Lord. In this way, the line between the secular and the sacred gets erased, and whatever profession or action we attempt becomes a divine mission. So we maintain our covenant in our temporal context, redeeming the time and working toward making our mark because he is at work in us.

The Jews recognized the first five books of Scripture as a summary of their covenant with God. We recognize the Bible in the same way; it is a divinely inspired abstract of God's relationship to mankind. It would be incredibly wise for us to understand, experience and apply its precepts and principles daily as we begin to view our covenant with our heavenly Father more seriously.

LIVING ON, HERE FOR THERE

Filmmaker Woody Allen has explored the big questions and issues of life. His musings are fascinatingly funny and depressing at the same time, and they often accurately reflect the secular questions of our society that never seem to find the sacred answers they're looking for. Allen once shared this sobering reflection (disguised in his usual wit):

> Someone once asked me if my dream was to live on in the hearts of my people. And I said, "I would like to live on in

my apartment." And that's really what I would prefer. . . .
You drop dead one day, and it means less than nothing if
billions of people are singing your praises every day, all day
long. I don't want to achieve immortality through my work.
I want to achieve it through not dying.[5]

This is from the same man who said, "I'm not afraid to die. I just
don't want to be there when it happens!"[6]

This is an intriguing observation, especially in a culture that
elevates celebrities to godlike status. But even the fame of most
celebrities will not outlive their generation. And then what?
Generations later, they'll be nothing more than names in someone's genealogical search, having become what we fear most—
forgotten and insignificant.

The Bible is the most countercultural book in the world and
always will be. We are not called to dilute it or make it relevant
to our culture, but rather we are called to follow it no matter
what our culture says. Thankfully, the Scriptures provide insight
about how we are to live in it. They reveal the kind of people we
are to be so that the light of God penetrates into the dark of the
temporal through us. *This gives us our significance: there is one
who promises we will never be forgotten.*

Practically speaking, the Scriptures work in combination with
God's Holy Spirit to guide us into truth every day. Such wisdom is
priceless. As Luke 16:14 says, even the most religious of people can
become scoffers, like the Pharisees who loved money and sought
to control rather than humbly living under the umbrella of grace.
To people who live like this, Jesus says, "You are the ones who
justify yourselves in the eyes of others, but God knows your hearts.
What people value highly is detestable in God's sight" (Luke 16:15).

If we're really good at impression management, people might
never really know the person we're hiding underneath. Still, we

will never be able to deceive God who knows our hearts. As we stare into the Scriptures we will find ourselves staring into a mirror that God uses to show us who we really are, how much he loves us and his great plan for redeeming us. Without this gift, we can begin to believe our own press. We can be so seduced by adulation and achievement that we begin to pursue these things that are really shadows over the invisible things that matter most.

One of the underlying revelations in Scripture is that our brief, earthly sojourn is the beginning of a much greater and ultimate citizenship with God. As a friend of mine puts it, we are called to live "here for there" or "now for then." This doesn't mean we are waiting until the day we die for our lives to begin to matter. Rather, our task is to bring the kingdom of God to earth in all that we do, so our choices, sacrifices and actions count and echo into eternity. The relationship we have with the Lord will become clearer after death, but so will our accountability for the way we have treated people publicly and privately on this earth.

Life on earth is not a game, nor is it merely some kind of prequel unrelated to the rest of our eternal life. We are actively living out the story of divine redemption, even now. As Jesus prayed, "Now this is eternal life: that they know you, the only true God, and Jesus Christ, whom you have sent" (John 17:3). For those of us who follow the Lord, our "eternal life" has already begun.

As Allen's comments remind us, death will one day greet us, and our chances to matter in *this life* will be gone. But it is on that day that all things will be tested by the fire of a holy God, and only the things that he declares worthwhile will matter. Until then, it would be wise for us to prepare for *then* by living our *now* in constant pursuit of a kingdom mentality and of the God of that kingdom himself, making use of the words he's given us to prepare for it.

You're Gonna Serve Somebody

It may be the devil or it may be the Lord,
but you're gonna have to serve somebody.

Bob Dylan

Bob Dylan's lyrics[7] resonate with the truth of Joshua 24:15: "If serving the LORD seems undesirable to you, then choose for yourselves this day whom you will serve." We've all got to make a choice. Serving Christ offers perfect freedom, and any other thing to which we commit our allegiance becomes enslavement. But we have to really understand this, and we may travel a long road before we know this as true by experience. We have been made by the Creator and exist to serve him—not to persuade him to serve us. The sooner we come to realize this, the sooner we can begin to make an eternal impression on the world while fastening our faith to him.

Like an anchor, an eternal perspective keeps us from drifting or going in a direction we shouldn't. Instead of living *egocentrically*, we can learn how to live *Christocentrically*. As Chinese pastor and author Watchman Nee says in *Christ the Sum of All Spiritual Things*, Christ is the center of all things, everything we want, everything we do and every impression we leave behind. This paradigm shift is essential, but just like the shift it took to lead us to salvation, it must completely renovate our point of view.

Unfortunately, this point of view can be reversed through the day-to-day stimuli of our world. The temporal will always attempt to pull us away from the eternal, causing us to flip back and forth between being self-centered and being Christ-centered, between living our own story or living in his. And we get deceived into thinking that we have a better idea of what's in our best interest.

The truth is, God always has our best interests at heart. When we understand this, we can begin to trust. Trust flows out of intimacy, and intimacy flows out of spending time with him. This may be difficult to practice at first, but it would be wise to avoid dwelling on our failed attempts and return to trying again to practice his presence through a variety of spiritual disciplines. (For an introduction to spiritual disciplines, you might like Richard J. Foster's *Celebration of Discipline* or John Ortberg's *The Life You've Always Wanted.*)

As we do, we will begin to understand the basis for trusting him and the unique platform he has given us to affect his world. By daily practicing our trust in him, we will realize that *whatever* he calls us to do is always in our best interest, even if it seems difficult or miniscule by our own personal measuring tape. The best way to start trusting him is by taking the time to invest in our relationship with him and with others. Other-centered relationships that express the love of Christ are the currency of heaven. When we reach out in Christlike humility, we walk in his footsteps and mark the pathway more permanently for those who follow behind us.

FOR FURTHER REFLECTION

1. How do you want to make your mark on this world?

2. Are you working now toward something that will last forever?

3. What does it mean to trust God like a skydiver trusts a parachute? What is this kind of trust? How does a person get it?

4. Reread the paragraph from the text of chapter 11 that begins, "Making a permanent mark in the world requires a radical perspective. . . ." What has been your experience of trying to know God by acquaintance—to truly know him?

5. Is there a lack of teaching in churches about how to come to know God by other means than just obedience and church attendance? What other ways can you know him experientially?

Scripture focus and practice. *Lectio divina* (sacred reading) is a spiritual exercise that Christian men and women have practiced since the sixth century. It does not replace traditional Bible study but instead looks at Scripture (rather than a text to be studied) as God's living word with the goal of a more intimate relationship. The four steps in *lectio divina* can be compared to eating.

Read a short text (take a bite)

- Find a quiet place and choose a short passage of Scripture. Read the passage several times slowly, as if you're walking through a new place and want to observe everything. If you don't know what passage to use, try a verse or two from something familiar such as Psalm 23 or the Lord's Prayer (Matthew 6:9-13).

Reflect (chew on the text)

- Spend time thinking about the text. Ask the Holy Spirit to use it to bring you closer to God. Visualize what you read; imagine experiencing it with all of your senses. See yourself with God in the story or text. Ask the Holy Spirit questions about it.

Respond (savor it)

- Practice talking to God about his Word. Did you see a promise in the text? Thank God for it. Are there words about who God is in the text? Pray the words back to him (Psalms are very good for this). If there is something challenging about the text, ask God to give you the courage to obey.

Rest (digest it)

- Be silent and comfortable. Listen. Focus on one word or short phrase from Scripture (for example, "shepherd" or "Our

Father" or "with me"). When your mind begins to wander, direct it back to God by focusing on your word or phrase. Allow God to use his Word to speak to you. Listen for his voice. Don't worry if you don't hear anything yet. You may hear something later. You may feel or sense his presence. You may feel peace or a conviction about something in your life that needs to be changed. Or you may first need to practice sitting silently before you begin to hear him. It takes discipline for people to sit still, but the rewards in terms of our relationship with God are well worth it.

For further guidance on the practice of spiritual reading, consider using my book *A Journal of Sacred Readings*. This one-year resource will enrich your encounters with Scripture by guiding you through the four-step process outlined above.

From Theology to Doxology

*Too many Christians come to church on
Sunday to rest at ease in Zion and across their
faces one seems to see as upon hotel room
doors, "Please Do Not Disturb."*

*It's not enough to be orthodox:
we must awaken to action.*

VANCE HAVNER

—〰—

D r. Vance Havner, a well-known revivalist with a flair for
painting vibrant word pictures, was right.[1] Once we have
embedded our story in God's greater story, we must live there.
Our Christianity must never be just a belief system; true faith
compels us to action.

If our presuppositions shape our priorities, and our priorities
shape our practice, then our practices reveal what our priorities
really are. Now that we are living in God's story, we have to act
like it, and our beliefs must manifest themselves in concrete,
tangible behavior. Our ethics must become our morality.

The true test of what we believe comes not in the all-too-sterile environment of the church but in the rough and tumble of the day-to-day. This is what the world sees. And if we profess to be followers of Jesus Christ but do not practice knowing him and conforming our lives to his image, we are deceived at best and deceivers at worst, poorly bearing the image of Christ to a watching world.

> Do not merely listen to the word, and so deceive yourselves. Do what it says. Anyone who listens to the word but does not do what it says is like someone who looks at his face in a mirror and, after looking at himself, goes away and immediately forgets what he looks like. But whoever looks intently into the perfect law that gives freedom, and continues in it—not forgetting what they have heard, but doing it—they will be blessed in what they do. . . .
>
> In the same way, faith by itself, if it is not accompanied by action, is dead. (James 1:22-25; 2:17)

While we cannot always tell the true condition of a person's heart from externals alone, there is still some merit in judging trees by their fruit. This is precisely what the world does when they come in contact with us whether we invite them to do so or not. The sad truth is that the world is fully aware of just how complacent and dishonest Christians often are with themselves (and others). In 2009, researchers at The Barna Group looked at a sample group of Christians from across the United States to determine what percentage of those who identify as Christians actually hold a biblical worldview. What they found, sadly, might not shock us: only 19 percent of Christians (fewer than one out of every five people who report that they follow Christ and believe they will one day go to heaven) actually hold a biblical worldview. Barna's work continues to study the impact of a person's worldview on his or her behavior. "Barna's research has discovered that there are unusually large differences in behavior related to matters such as media use, profanity, gambling, alcohol use, honesty, civility, and sexual choices."[2]

Ron Sider, in his book *The Scandal of the Evangelical Conscience*, goes on to say:

> Scandalous behavior is rapidly destroying American Christianity. By their daily activity, most "Christians" regularly commit treason. With their mouths they claim that Jesus is Lord, but with their actions they demonstrate allegiance to money, sex, and self-fulfillment.[3]

The hard truth is that we're going to have to become much more serious about examining our presuppositions and priorities, and we're going to have to start *living these priorities out in our practice* before the world can ever see our true faith and the reflection of the one in whom we place it.

God gives us opportunities to share his message, but we often miss them. The 1999 movie *The Matrix* is about freedom fighters entering the matrix to save people enslaved by a false reality—a perfect opportunity to talk about how Christ rescues those enslaved by sin. The 2004 movie *The Passion of Christ* provided another chance to talk to people about Jesus. Tragic events such as 9/11, mass school shootings across America and the deadly terrorist attacks on Paris, not to mention all of the earthquakes, hurricanes and forest fires around the world, provide opportunities to talk with friends and neighbors. Dystopian novels and movies such as *The Hunger Games* and *Divergent* open up discussions about worldviews. We have countless opportunities to use temporal things to draw attention to eternal truths. But most of us miss them. Why aren't we examining our faith in light of what is going on in our world? Why aren't we talking about pain and true healing in times when people suffer? Why aren't we asking people why dystopian novels are so popular and telling people why eternity is a far more interesting story? It seems that the world is awakening to its spiritual hunger just as the church is putting on its pajamas and drifting off to sleep. *Perhaps it is not the unsaved who are most in need of a spiritual awakening.*

In previous chapters, we examined how presuppositions can shape our perspective and rank our priorities. Now the pedal hits the metal as we move into the arena of practical living, out of the ethereal and into ground-level application. Jesus rarely minced his words. When he said a tree could be recognized by its fruit, he was getting at the root: *if you don't live it, then you don't really believe it.*

APOLOGISTS AND APOSTLES

We have more apologists than apostles. Too many
Christians are sound—sound asleep!

VANCE HAVNER

What is an apologist?[4] The word comes from the Greek word *apologia*, which means a defense of the faith in the face of an accusation. Surely we need apologists to speak away the mountains of errors that have sprung up. We need to answer those who denounce absolutes and question whether it's possible to believe in anything. We *must* defend the Christian faith and prove, by reason, that there is *real* reason to believe and a real *One* to believe *in*.

But what happens when we spend all of our time defending and none of our time demonstrating that truth? We've all heard "You can talk the talk, but can you walk the walk?" Faith with feet—this is an apostle. The first twelve were chosen by Jesus and sent out to do his will and preach his message. The word *apostle* grew to mean anyone bringing Christianity to a new country or region. Maybe we can make that definition more broad. We have been commissioned by Christ and sent to carry the message of Christ to where we are. We have been chosen to represent him (2 Corinthians 5:20)! Without real-life, wide-awake apostles, the world may hear the truth over and over but will never *see a living truth* that shows hope is real.

As the postmodern age has emerged out of the modern era, the need to clarify and communicate the truth claims of our faith has never been greater. But if we are really living in a time when stories, images and relationships are preferred over pronouncements of propositional truth, then the biggest need is for those outside the community of faith to hear the story of Jesus after they've seen it lived out in our lives. Rather than merely speaking words, we must *embody* the words of Scripture every day!

In *The Mark of the Christian*, theologian Francis Schaeffer said that love is the ultimate apologetic. Evangelist Dwight L. Moody famously said, "Out of one hundred men, one will read the Bible; the other ninety-nine will read the Christian." The Bible is full of comparable encouragements to become more like Jesus in order to challenge people's perceptions of our faith. Godly patterns of living can correct false perceptions of Christianity without a word.

It's a lot like this: in a small town, one irresponsible person can ruin a good family's name. When this happens, members of that family may move away or change their names. It takes a bold person to remain at home and live an upright life so he can redeem his family. Sadly, we must admit that there have been many irresponsible Christians bringing shame on our family. But surely what we need is not to move away or give ourselves new names. What we need is more courage to stand up and live the lives we were called to live in order to redeem the name of the church in our world, starting in our own hometown.

We cannot control people's perceptions of us, but it is within our grasp to continue to live out our faith by our priorities, expressed in our practice. The transforming power of Jesus Christ can turn us into real-life stories of redemption.

SETTING THE WORLD ON FIRE

Our theology needs to go up in doxology.
We have the facts, but not the fire.

If we had as much vitality as we have had vocality,
we would have set the world on fire long ago.

VANCE HAVNER[5]

Sometime during the winter of 1941, a cold and hungry Jewish woman knocked on the door of a Protestant pastor named Andre Trocmé. She was looking for food and shelter and the pastor's family took her in. Her knock and Trocmé's answer sparked a bonfire-sized response from the small French mountain village where he was pastor.

The Christians in Le Chambon-sur-Lignon were a quiet people whose actions spoke much louder than their words. Led by Pastor Trocmé, they began what has been called a "conspiracy of goodness" between 1941 and 1945. For them, there was no other choice. They didn't know about the Nazi death camps yet, but they knew the Nazis had said publicly that they were creating a special city just for the Jews. The thought of delivering up another human being for any reason was impossible for this group to bear.

By some estimates, collaborators in occupied France delivered eighty-three thousand Jews to Nazi death camps. But the ordinary, poor people of Le Chambon took people into their homes and quietly saved a population of people as large as their own village. "No one in Le Chambon ever turned away, denounced or betrayed a single Jewish refugee."[6] They saved the lives of five thousand people and inspired even more.

The villagers didn't hide Jews in their walls, attics or sheds. The Jews lived with them; their children were educated together; they ate together. This was the right thing to do, and they were going to do it. Soon they were protecting so many people that it was impossible for them *not* to be found out.

> The refugees were welcomed without hesitation. They were housed in private homes, on farms as well as in public institutions and were hidden in the countryside whenever the Nazis came through. One of the villagers later recalled: "As soon as the soldiers left, we would go into the forest and sing a song. When they heard that song, the Jews knew it was safe to come home."[7]

In the summer of 1942, two French police buses came to the village to take the refugees away. Pastor Trocmé refused to give the police the names of the Jews in his village, and the buses left without any prisoners.

Trocmé was eventually arrested but was later released, despite having refused to sign a commitment to cooperate with the Vichy government. Several months later, he took his rescue operation underground when there were rumors of potential re-arrest. His nephew, who had opened a children's home for Jewish orphans, was sent to a Nazi death camp and killed. Now led by Trocmé's wife, the Jews in Le Chambon remained in relative peace until the war ended, having been prayed for, fed and cared for by people who saw them only as fellow human beings in need.

During a 1990 ceremony honoring the village, it was said, "The village was unique in that almost all the people of the plateau were involved in saving these Jews, and no one said a word."[8] With little vocality but lots of vitality, the people of Le Chambon-sur-Lignon sang their praises to God to the tune of five thousand lives.

> Doxology
> [dok-**sol**-*uh*-jee]
> noun
> 1. a hymn or form of words containing an ascription of praise to God

What would our world look like if we all assumed Christian responsibility like the villagers of Le Chambon, seeing it as our duty to live out our praise to God by service to his people? Our theology must become manifest in our actions if we are going to make any difference at all. The ability to gather biblical data and form divine conclusions will win us few followers if there is not a mysterious-but-visible overflow of Christ's life in ours. Without an active relationship with the Lord, we may have the facts, but we will never have the fire.

DEFENDING, DEMONSTRATING, DIETING AND THE NEED FOR DISCIPLINE

We have talked much further along than we have walked.
We need to let our feet catch up with our tongues. We defend the
truth, but we do not demonstrate the truth. We ponder it
instead of proving it. We preach a dynamite
gospel and live firecracker lives.

VANCE HAVNER

We say that the Lord is our number one priority in life, but aren't we often more concerned with our selves than with our Savior?[9] Some preach that if you want to know your real priorities, you can take a look at your checkbook and your calendar; this is not a bad place to start. You may truly believe intellectually, but has the power of Christ *gripped your life*? Is it changing what you do? Is it evident to everyone around that you live for Jesus?

A theoretical or intellectual faith is deceptive primarily because on the surface it looks like real faith. It's like the story of a guy whose wife asked him to carve their Thanksgiving turkey. He takes out a guidebook, grabs the knife and prepares to cut, thinking he is ready. But he doesn't know what to do next because his turkey doesn't have dotted lines on it like the one in the guidebook. In the same way, if we merely read the Bible as theory then we miss the point, and we will not be prepared for the days God calls us to. The Bible is meant to be applied in real-life situations. If you asked someone who had only read a guidebook about swimming, "Do you know how to swim?" he'd say, "Of course I know how to swim. I read the book." But if you asked him, "Can you swim?" he'd have to say, "I've never tried."

Tim Hansel wrote a very practical and intriguing little book called *When I Relax I Feel Guilty*. In it, he describes what he calls the trap of "Almost Christianity."

Almost Christianity will reveal itself in countless subtle ways. I know many who claim that with Christ all things are possible, except to help them lose weight. I know those who extol the benefits of quiet time but don't have enough time for contemplation themselves. Others lecture on the resurrection and try to do everything on their own power. I know people who give sermons on the Lordship of Christ but who can't slow down because they think the world

would collapse without their activities. Some people applaud the security we have in Christ but are unwilling to
take any chances. And still others glorify the freedom that
is ours but are still enslaved to their work.[10]

Is our work, time and even our diet the business of the Holy
Spirit? Is Jesus the Lord over how we treat our family members
and what we watch on TV? Ouch! It's easier for us to compart-
mentalize and assume some things are not his business. But then
we are failing to bring *all* areas of our lives under the lordship of
Christ.

Our faith demands and requires application in all areas of our
life. The Bible was not merely written to *inform* us but to
transform every area of our lives. What does this look like? How
are we transformed? How do we bring it down to the everyday?

If you want to learn a language or to become more skillful in
a sport, you practice, train and form new habits. At first these
things may not be very enjoyable, but after a while, they become
second nature as you develop your skills.

But there's a choice that must be made. While it's never too
late to learn a musical instrument, if you're going to pick up a
trumpet when you're fifty, you're not going to play like Miles
Davis on the first or even the one-hundred-fiftieth try. You have
to first devote yourself to the discipline of it. What do you want?
What is the price? Are you willing to pay it? The time you spend
on that practice is time you will *not* spend on something else.
And you can't do everything; you must choose.

Similarly, there is a price to be paid for following God. We
may assume that a crash diet of a week of quiet times or a month
of perfect church attendance is all we need for a quick fix and
healthy relationship with Jesus. We can add new Christian habits
to our lives, and this is good, but the discipline of practicing

these habits over time is the essential part. Dietary supplements can be good, but they cannot replace a steady diet of healthy foods. Discipline produces results in the long game.

God has called us to make decisions and create habits that are pleasing to him so that by lifting up his name we, and those we know, are drawn to him. But these choices have to manifest themselves in our everyday lives. We can't run away to a mountain retreat, come back with an "improved" relationship with God and expect that we've taken care of the spiritual portion of our lives. Truth doesn't change our lives until we start putting it to use all the time. Developing a new habit of Bible study and prayer but failing to apply what it says to your life would be like buying a couple of gallons of paint at The Home Depot and leaving it in the garage. It's not going to change the way people see your house until you do the work of actually putting the paint on the walls.

In June of 1986, I had the privilege of meeting a man named Mark Pett who was in vocational ministry, just like me. Unlike me, though, he had terminal cancer and had been given six months to live. He saw every minute he had on earth as a privilege. His paradigm fully embraced the ideas we've discussed in this book. We were the same age, but Mark had gained an extraordinary measure of wisdom through the pain he experienced. I took notes whenever I met with him. Here is some of what he said that day in June:

> We have a clear sense of birth but a theoretical sense of death. Understand that you have a certain number of days. There is no good time to die. You don't retire from life and get ready for death. When you leave this planet, you will never again have the privilege of sharing the gospel, serving the lost, feeding the poor. This is not a guilt trip

but a reminder to enjoy the opportunity and privilege of representing Christ to the world. The love you give back to him drives the opportunities you have. . . . We must not just wait to get to heaven but relish the opportunities we only have now.

These words marked me, as did these thoughts Mark shared during a second visit we had in March of 1987:

I am trying to come to grips on a daily basis with what it means to seek first his kingdom. Part of this means not pursuing what our system rewards. There is a problem of drifting back into complacency. God has not promised me tomorrow. There are things to accomplish on this side, and it takes a measure of faith to believe that there is something on the other.

Although Mark probably stood about 6 feet 2 inches tall normally, he was about 5 feet 8 inches tall at the time of our last visit. His body was basically crumbling from the cancer, creating difficulty for him to even go down stairs without great agony. Yet because of the pain he'd endured, he had outstripped me in wisdom.

Mark found a way to defy the doctor's prognosis and lived a good deal longer than the six months he was given. He went to be with the Lord in February of 1988. A friend of mine, Larry Moody, shared this key insight at Mark's funeral:

If you would have asked me when I first met Mark what he was like, I would have said he was a gifted man. But in the last three years if you'd asked me . . . I would say he was a godly man.

It's one thing to minister out of your gifts and knowledge base, and it's another thing to minister out of your experience of pain, neediness and dependence upon God. Even on our best days we don't have any assurance of how long we will be here. Mark stressed the privilege of practice and the window of opportunity we have to make a difference with the time we have right now.

If our practice doesn't include things like time in Scripture and time in prayer, cherishing the opportunities we have to serve other people, time talking with our Father and time in reflection, then there's something wrong with our priorities. A life without these things is not destined for transformation. You simply cannot be transformed into the image of Jesus without the diligent work of spiritual discipline.

ETERNITY AND NOW

It is my suspicion, though, that what we call discipline on earth will be our pleasure in heaven. Prayer and talking to God will be more fully realized in our resurrected body and state than we can now imagine. Perhaps even the Scriptures will take on new meaning in light of the thousands of things we cannot comprehend until then. All of this unmediated and direct interaction will create a relationship like no relationship we have ever known.

But for now, we live here. And my friend Mark made me realize this important fact about being alive on earth. There are really only two things that you can do here that you will never have the opportunity to do in heaven: share the good news with those who do not have it and serve people who are in need. We would do well to treasure these opportunities. The days are short. We can all be involved in sharing the good news with our lives and our witness. We can preach a message simply by our integrity and the diligence with which we work. We can follow the statement often attributed to St. Francis of Assisi: "Preach the gospel always; if necessary, use words." God has given us an arena of influence and opportunities—*and it matters tremendously how we view these things.* We are living in his story now; what will we do with the chapters he is giving us?

In the life of Jesus, we see no evidence of a dichotomy between the sacred and the secular, the eternal and the temporal. The Lord lived on this earth in such a way that all things took on the eternal, from the object lessons in his teaching to the scandalous lives he redeemed. Jesus perfectly explained and exemplified the kingdom of heaven. Perhaps it was his unique insight into both that allowed him to be the bridge between the two, showing us things about eternity that we could never dream.

A good friend of mine is fond of asking, "What are you taking under your arm to the ultimate show and tell?" There will one day be a show and tell that takes place before the judgment seat of Christ. This particular ruling is not a verdict of condemnation but one of rewards where we give an account for ourselves and receive recognition accordingly. The Scriptures tell us that we will be so humbled by it all that we will literally cast any rewards back toward the feet of the Lord in recognition of who he is.

God is God, and we are not. He is sovereign and has given each of us just enough time on this planet to accomplish his purposes for us. We need neither one second more nor one second less. Our last years may well be the key years of our lives, and yet all the chapters of our stories will have led up to those moments, converging in such a way that, no matter where we find ourselves now, we may finish well. For now and for then, our theology can go up in a doxology that goes something like this:

> Now to him who is able to do immeasurably more than all we ask or imagine, according to his power that is at work within us, to him be glory in the church and in Christ Jesus throughout all generations, for ever and ever! Amen. (Ephesians 3:20-21)

FOR FURTHER REFLECTION

1. What was said in chapter 1 about fixing a broken story? How does it happen?

2. This chapter talks about a "constant pursuit of a kingdom mentality." What do you think that is? What choices would it require?

3. What words from the Bible come to mind when you think of preparing for eternity? (Can't think of any? Ask a spiritual mentor.)

4. What Scripture have you read lately that demands to be acted upon? Have you done it? Talk to someone about this.

5. If you're under the age of thirty-five, in what ways is communication among your generation different from how your parents communicate? How important are stories, images and relationships compared to pronouncements of propositional truth?

Scripture focus. Read James 1:22-25 and 2:17. Consider copying it and keeping it somewhere you will see it often.

Practice. As a Christian, it is your job to tell the story of Jesus and to share your own story. This is the beginning of evangelism. Take a moment to write two stories and practice sharing them with people around you.

First, write about Jesus. Reach all the way back into Genesis 1–3 with the creation of humans and the fall of man in the garden. Think about including ideas from John 1, which says Jesus was there with God in the beginning of time, or what you learned from Colossians 1:16. Tell who Jesus was since the beginning, how he came to earth and, more importantly, why. Tell how he died and what his death and resurrection accomplished for you and for everyone. Tell what you know of our future with him. If you have difficulty telling this whole story, consider asking for help from a spiritual mentor.

The second story is yours. Did you find yourself in a broken story? How did you learn about and believe in Jesus? What difference has it made in your life so far? How has your thinking changed? What do you hope for? It's okay if you're still thinking through these questions yourself. It's always more important to be honest about where you are in your story.

Epilogue

—⟋⟋⟋—

The things I've taught in this book are seen in the larger-than-life story of my friend and mentor Charles "Chuck" Colson. I can't think of a better example of how God redeemed a broken story. What God did for Chuck, he can do for you too. This is the short version, but if you're interested in reading more of Chuck's story, check out his autobiography, *Born Again*, or *Seven Men: And the Secret of Their Greatness* by Eric Metaxas (the other stories in that book are also well worth your time).

Chuck's story—both the worst and best parts of it—happened in the public eye. Chuck achieved the heights of worldly power and publicly hit rock bottom, then became known worldwide again for how God powerfully used him. Not every story will be this dramatic or public, yet any story God redeems is glorious. And God does not weigh the value of a life by the amount of recognition it receives. Throughout the course of history, God has been rewriting the story of those he redeems, turning broken lives around. The thread of redemption leading to a radically changed perspective from the temporal to the eternal has been happening both loudly and quietly for all of human history and will continue to do so—maybe even for you.

—⟨⟨⟩⟩—

It was August 12, 1973, and it was hot. Chuck sat in his car near the driveway of the Massachusetts home of Tom Phillips, president of the multimillion dollar Raytheon Company. With his face in his hands and his forehead on the steering wheel, Chuck—a man known for toughness and ruthlessness—cried hard. Things had not gone as he had expected. He hadn't suspected that meeting with Phillips would break him.

Truth be told, he was broken before that summer evening. In March of that year, he'd been forced to resign as special counsel for the White House due to the Watergate scandal. So in August, Chuck and his wife, Patty, left their home in Virginia for a much-needed getaway from the cruel headlines, questioning and almost daily media ambushes.

Chuck had last met with Phillips in March. When Chuck practiced law prior to joining the Nixon administration in 1969, his firm had represented Raytheon, the largest employer in New England. Just after his forced resignation, Chuck—eager to rebuild his practice—went to Brainerd Holmes, Raytheon's vice president. Holmes took him to see Phillips but with a warning: "[Phillips] has had quite a change—some sort of religious experience."[1]

Phillips didn't mention anything about his experience when he met with Chuck; he just seemed different. Phillips was compassionate and gentle, and he wanted to know how Chuck was doing. Chuck asked him directly about the experience Holmes had mentioned. Yes, Phillips said. He had accepted Jesus Christ and committed his life to him.[2]

Though this kind of language is familiar to many people today, it was not familiar to Chuck, and it left him confused and uncomfortable. Chuck knew about Jesus Christ, but "accepting him" and "committing his life" to him? These phrases sounded strange. Still, Phillips had Chuck's attention and explained that he'd gotten to the point where he felt empty. He said his life wasn't worth anything and meeting Jesus had changed everything—his values, attitudes and whole life.

Chuck didn't want to admit it, but he felt empty too. After dedicating his whole self to the cause of getting Richard Nixon reelected, he was hurt when Nixon asked him to resign over the Watergate scandal.[3] Over the course of the summer, Chuck had faced a series of public humiliations, false accusations (along with some that were true) and crushing blows. Chuck knew he had committed crimes and used unethical tactics to deal with the president's "enemies" (of whom Chuck kept a list—along with their weaknesses and incriminating facts about them). Now the Senate Select Committee on Special Campaign Activities was making public all of the private conversations recorded in Nixon's office, and pressure was building. Chuck wasn't guilty of all they were accusing him, but he was guilty, and he could feel it.[4]

When the Committee recessed in August, Chuck and Patty eagerly escaped the pressure of Washington. They stopped in Massachusetts to visit Phillips and his wife, who warmly welcomed them and served ice tea. Phillips invited Chuck out to his screened porch. Phillips shared about how coming to know and trust Jesus Christ had changed everything and given meaning to a life that had felt empty. Chuck thought Phillips seemed more alive than he had ever seen him.

Even his confrontations seemed genuinely gentle and caring. Phillips said that Chuck had played dirty to get Nixon reelected, even though Nixon would have won the election anyway. He said that whether Chuck was guilty or not, running a campaign by those tactics was wrong, and Chuck should have known that.

"Don't you understand that?" Phillips asked, less accusing and more compassionate, trying to make Chuck see what he had previously not even considered. "Chuck," he said, "I don't think you will understand what I'm saying about God until you are willing to face yourself honestly. . . ."[5]

Phillips picked up C. S. Lewis's *Mere Christianity* and began to read:

> There is one vice of which no man in the world is free; of which everyone in the world loathes when he sees it in someone else; and of which hardly any people, except Christians, ever imagine that they are guilty themselves. . . . There is no fault . . . which we are more unconscious of in ourselves. And the more we have it in ourselves, the more we dislike it in others.
>
> The vice I am talking about is Pride. . . . Pride leads to every other vice: it is the complete anti-God state of mind.

Phillips continued to read. Red-faced and his heart burning, Chuck could feel the conviction.

> In God, you come up against something which is in every respect immeasurably superior to yourself. Unless you know God as that—and, therefore, know yourself as nothing in comparison—you do not know God at all. As long as you are proud, you do not know God at all.[6]

In his autobiography, *Born Again*, Chuck said he felt "naked and unclean" at that moment, all his defenses exposed.[7] Chuck sipped the iced tea to cool himself and to swallow the emotions that were welling up as his friend read on, "Pride is spiritual cancer: it eats up the very possibility of love, or contentment, or even common sense."[8]

As a dying man sees his life flash in events before his eyes, so Chuck saw moments he hadn't thought of in years—his prep school graduation speech, his choice of Brown over Harvard—with one common theme at the center: his pride. He remembered striving to enter the Marines for the sake of country—and pride. He had clawed for position in politics longing to hear the words, "Mr. Colson, the President wants to see you. . . ." He remembered harsh words he'd said jokingly, actions taken for wrong reasons and the collapse of his first marriage. Pride, Chuck realized, had been the primary motivating factor in his life and a shield that had kept him from caring about others. Lewis's words were ripping through what he'd worn like armor for the first forty-two years of his life.[9]

But Phillips didn't leave it there. He gave Chuck the book and read him some encouraging passages from Psalms, including Psalm 37:3-4: "Trust in the Lord and do good . . . and he will give you the desires of your heart." Phillips shared words from the Gospel of John 3 about how a man can be born again. And he prayed for him. Chuck had never heard anyone pray like that—like God was sitting right there in the room.

Chuck took the book, thanked Phillips and his wife for their hospitality and left. He had held back the tears on the screened porch, but by the time he was out of their driveway, he was crying so hard he couldn't see. Phillips had asked Chuck if he wanted to pray too, but he had declined. He wasn't ready, he had said. Now he longed to go back into the house and pray, but the lights were out. He couldn't go back.[10]

Chuck stopped the car and cried hard; it felt like water was washing over him. And then he felt something sudden and strange: relief and a desire to surrender. He was not committing his life to Christ, but he was surrendering. The commitment would come. "Take me," Chuck said over and over in the car. It was all he could say.[11]

Chuck and Patty left Massachusetts for Maine and found a vacation spot in a quiet coastal area where few people recognized him. The television was broken at the inn where they stayed—a gift from God! No one there would hear terrible news reports about him; he and Patty could find some rest. He began to read *Mere Christianity* the way he would prepare for a case, taking notes with a legal pad and pen. Chuck had surrendered, but there were questions to be answered—fundamental questions—and his mind could not accept Jesus without more information.[12]

Chuck spent the entire vacation in this research. Is there a God? If God is real and good, why is there evil in the world? What is free will? Who is God, and who am I in relation to him? Patty asked him, "What's in that book you're reading?"[13] The answer was simple: everything that was missing in his life. By the end of his vacation, Chuck joined his story with God's: "Lord Jesus, I believe you. I accept you. Please come into my life. I commit it to you."

Then Chuck changed. Everyone who was close to him (and even some who had not known him closely) saw the difference. Not everyone who is transformed by Christ changes in such a dramatic way, but that's how Chuck's story went. He was an entirely new man. He had bullied his way through much of life, willing to do anything for what he believed—even if it was unethical or unkind. The strengths of his old life were his passion and loyalty. He still had them, but they had a different focus now. He no longer served Nixon or even himself—he served Christ. And when the object of one's loyalty changes from an earthly master to the eternal God, that paradigm shift affects everything.

His affiliations began to change in remarkable ways. This shift continued the day Doug Coe showed up in Chuck's law office.

Coe was the leader of the National Prayer Breakfast and of the Fellowship, a discreet Washington Bible study group filled with political leaders with connections around the country and the world. Though Coe entered Chuck's office a total stranger, Chuck prayed his first prayers aloud with Coe that day. At the end of their meeting, Coe handed him a Bible with a note inside that contained a quote from Senate Chaplain Peter Marshall: "To Charles—it is better to fail in a cause that will ultimately succeed than to succeed in a cause that will ultimately fail."[14] Chuck's story was being rewritten.

Though most of Chuck's friends had been avoiding him since Watergate, Coe told him there were men and women all over Washington praying for him and ready to help. Chuck was not alone. There was "a veritable underground of Christ's men all throughout the government."[15] And they began to call him to offer their support.

One of the fundamental benefits of joining in Christ's story is that, by doing so, you're joining with many companions. What has been called the "fellowship of the saints" is real and a comfort so great that it is nearly impossible to explain to someone who has not experienced it. People who had been Chuck's enemies were now his brothers. And he would need them.

Not everyone who commits his life to Christ is immediately forced to see his sins publicized, but that is what happened next for Chuck. He had been a Christian for only days when he was thrown back into the Watergate scandal. He went through the steps: a grand jury investigation and then indictment. Newspapers daily featured his name. The media literally camped out in his front yard. The White House was in turmoil, and Chuck, as Nixon's former aide and ongoing confidante, was at the center of the storm.

Congressman Al Quie remembers how he witnessed a miracle in Chuck's life when Chuck was invited to his Washington home to meet some other Christians. Chuck, the ruthless defender of the cause of conservatism, was sitting in the living room across from the most liberal senator any of them had ever known— Harold Hughes, who was known for getting up and walking out of the Senate when a Republican stood up to speak. Coe had arranged the meeting with a reticent Hughes. When Hughes said there was no one he disliked more than Chuck (Hughes had been on the enemies list Chuck made), Quie told him that he was being un-Christlike.[16] Quie remembers the other guests questioning Chuck about his recent and extraordinary conversion, which happened at a time when a distraction from his illegal actions would have been the perfect political move. Was his conversion genuine?

Chuck was about to go to jail, and he deserved to go to jail. But his concern at Quie's house that night was not his impending imprisonment. As the Christian leaders grilled him, Chuck's answers seemed sincere. "What worries me," Quie remembers Chuck saying, "is that, if it is not for real, what will that do to Jesus Christ?"[17] Hughes was sitting across the room when Chuck said those words. Hughes threw his hands in the air and stood up. "Chuck," he said, "if you've accepted Christ into your life— and I believe you have—I am your brother for life." The senator embraced Chuck and the two became lifelong friends.[18]

Others from the Fellowship began to surround Chuck too. They prayed *for* him daily and *with* him regularly. There were so many of them that Chuck was shocked. People he had known and respected for years were believers, quietly living out their faith in their government positions. Chuck needed their support. The old Chuck and all his pride were dying away—being demolished, actually—but not without a great deal of pain.[19]

The indictment process dragged on during the summer of 1973 and through the fall. At the beginning of 1974, Watergate special prosecutor Leon Jaworski offered Chuck a plea bargain. Under the deal, Chuck would be charged with only a misdemeanor and allowed to continue his law practice if he would just admit to one charge: conspiring to break into the office of Daniel Ellsberg's psychiatrist.

Ellsberg was responsible for leaking the Pentagon Papers, a classified report of US political and military actions in Vietnam. Though the report didn't exactly incriminate Nixon, it did incriminate the two presidents who preceded him, and Nixon would soon be up for reelection to that office. Not only that, though it wasn't in the report, Nixon had escalated the conflict in Vietnam and Cambodia while publicly promising to bring troops home and end the war. After Ellsberg submitted the papers to the *New York Times* and they began publishing excerpts, Nixon aides wanted to paint Ellsberg as mentally unstable in order to discredit him.

But Chuck hadn't known about the break-in until after it had happened. The offer of a misdemeanor instead of a felony charge was tempting, but to plead guilty to something he had not done was just another form of lying. So on March 1, 1974, just as it looked like the judge might be preparing to dismiss the charges against him, Chuck and his lawyers asked the judge to allow him to plead guilty to obstruction of justice—a felony.[20]

On June 21, Chuck received a sentence of up to three years in prison and a $5,000 fine. In July, he entered the Fort Holabird Detention Center in Maryland and then moved to Maxwell Federal Prison Camp in Alabama.

Chuck's Fellowship brothers had told him, "If you're indicted, we're indicted with you." His client Dusty Miller from the Teamsters had said almost the same thing.[21] But in prison, it was just Chuck and Jesus and the way he would find Jesus was in the Scriptures. Chuck took to serious Bible study. One day, he read

Hebrews 2:11: "Both the one who makes people holy and those who are made holy are of the same family. So Jesus is not ashamed to call them brothers and sisters." Jesus was not afraid to call Chuck "brother." Neither would Chuck be afraid to call those around him brothers. The words of that Scripture sank in deep. He began trying to see life from the perspective of the prisoners at Maxwell. This last blow to his pride was a little easier, and he began to serve by mopping floors and washing laundry for his fellow inmates.

Chuck's imprisonment was part of something bigger, and he knew it. Prison was not a waste of his precious time; God was using this time to teach Chuck the life that would lead to his redemption. He began looking for other believers to form a fellowship inside the walls of Maxwell; most rejected him. But after he and another passionate Christian prayed for the parole of another prisoner—and the parole was granted—others began to join. Chuck led a Bible study and, against the advice from his law partners, helped an illiterate prisoner with a letter to a judge about his parole.

But life in prison was not easy, even for a person of faith. Chuck was dragged in and out of Maxwell for more testimony in court, though he desperately wanted to be done with the Watergate scandal. Nixon received a pardon from President Ford in September of 1974. Chuck expected and even campaigned for the same. For a time, that eternal perspective seemed to be slipping away as he reverted to his old tactics, asking others to badger Ford into granting it. The pardon never came. At the end of 1974, Chuck's father died while he was still in prison, and Chuck sank into depression.[22] When three others involved in Watergate were released early, Chuck and his family thought maybe he would finally be released. But it didn't happen.

Meanwhile, the Virginia State Supreme Court had ruled to disbar him. He would have no career upon his return. And as if all of this weren't enough, in January of 1975 Chuck learned that his son Christian had been arrested at the University of South Carolina and charged with possession of marijuana with intent to distribute. UPI news reported that, upon his arrest, the young man identified himself and said, "Now you've got us both."[23]

By this time, Chuck was one of only two Watergate defendants still in prison. Patty was suffering deeply from the pain of watching others released while her husband was still incarcerated, and now her son was also imprisoned. So deep was the Colson family's pain that Chuck's friend Quie offered himself in Chuck's place after he found an obscure statute that said a congressman could take the place of a federal prisoner with presidential permission. Chuck was touched but turned down Quie's proposal.[24]

On January 29, 1975, Chuck was at a very low point. He had no idea that his Fellowship brothers sensed it and were praying for him at that very moment to hand everything to God. Chuck somehow heard their prayers and did just that. "Lord, if this is what it is all about, then I thank you. I praise you for leaving me in prison. . . ." Chuck was convinced he would serve the full three years of his sentence, but suddenly he felt strangely free.[25]

To everyone's surprise, when the judge on Chuck's case learned about his son's arrest, the judge released him, citing "family problems" that necessitated his release. On January 31, 1975, just two days after surrendering to God about staying, Chuck was set free from prison having served only seven months of his three-year sentence. On the drive home he told Patty, "From now on, life will be different."[26] He was right.

Chuck was back at Maxwell Prison only a week later, this time as a visitor. He had promised that he would not forget the friends he'd made there. This visit was the first of a million proofs that he meant it.[27]

After some months of indecision and frustration about what he would do with the rest of his life, Chuck received a vision from God. Looking in the mirror one morning, he no longer saw himself. Instead, he saw prison inmates carrying Bibles, studying together and praying. The vision lasted only a few seconds, but that was all it took. His friend Eric Metaxas says that although Chuck was not the kind of Christian (then or after) to talk about mystical experiences, Chuck could not deny what had happened that day.[28]

So he responded to the calling God had given him: rehabilitate prisoners and reform the prison system. Through Senator Hughes, Chuck became friends with the director of federal prisons, who approved his plan.[29]

Within three years, Chuck's Prison Fellowship was in six hundred prisons in twenty-three states. The ministry soon spread to other countries and spawned other organizations. Despite the fact that many in Washington still disbelieved the authenticity of his conversion, Chuck continued to go about the work God had given him. He became known as not only a rehabilitator of prisoners and a reformer of the prison system but also a defender of the weak in general. He welcomed lepers in India. He worked to spur the White House to end war in Sudan, fight sex trafficking and help those dealing with the global spread of AIDS.

He was a new man at home too. His son, who expected a lecture that first week after his father was released from prison, received encouragement instead. His daughter Emily described a softness that came over her father and said that, though he was extremely busy (as before), the new Chuck would drop everything to be "fully present" for his family. Later, this would become especially true with his autistic grandson, Max.[30]

Friends noticed how Chuck would forgive others even though he had often not received forgiveness himself. It took Chuck three decades to convince some people that his conversion was real, but it took him only days to start seeking forgiveness and offering it to others.

Chuck worked as hard after meeting Christ as he did before but with a totally different aim and perspective. By anyone's measure, his accomplishments after his conversion were far greater than those in his first forty-two years of life. He mobilized Christians around the nation and around the world to minister to prisoners and their families. He worked with Justice Fellowship to pass legislation to help stop prison rape. He established scholarships for released prisoners.

Chuck's ministry went far beyond the prison scene, seeking to equip and edify the entire body of believers so they would learn to see their lives through an eternal lens. Chuck was naturally eloquent and learned early on to explain his own faith. But he wanted believers everywhere to develop an eternal perspective—and the ability to articulate it. He founded the Colson Center for Christian Worldview, which teaches and trains leaders to affect culture. He worked to bring evangelical Christians and Catholics together. His books *Born Again, How Now Shall We Live?* and *The Faith* helped bring people to faith, teaching the historical truths of that faith and how to live them out.

He worked so hard that his family would joke about it. He would tell them all, "Okay, let's all relax for five minutes." Six minutes, he said, would be wasteful.[31] In March of 2012, Chuck fell ill while giving a speech and died less than a month later. At his funeral, a prison chaplain who had once been an inmate himself described Chuck as "a friend of sinners," like Jesus.[32] Though many offered kind words upon his death, these words of

Senator Mitch McConnell are especially poignant: "He lives on
as a modern model of redemption and a permanent rebuttal to
the cynical claim that there are no second chances in life."[33]

The reach of Chuck's ministry and the richness of his legacy
are so great and so diverse that they can no longer be measured,
nor have they reached their limits. All of the organizations and
programs he began continue today.

—ₘₒₒ—

Your sins may not be making headlines. You may not be on your
way to jail. You don't have to be publicly shamed to join God's
story. All you need is to recognize your sin and emptiness
without him and trust him to lead you into something better.
Few people will accomplish as much as Chuck did after his conversion. Most people don't have the same kinds of opportunities
he did. But how much you accomplish isn't what matters to God.
What matters is what you make of the opportunities he gives you,
and more importantly the focus of your heart while you do it.

Everyone has a broken story, and everyone has a choice. The
pain of our brokenness can lead us into despair and emptiness,
or it can cause us to examine what we believe so that we can
ultimately experience true and lasting redemption.

When our story is set in an eternal context, everything
changes, just like it did for my friend Chuck. It starts with a
simple prayer like his: "Lord Jesus, I believe you. I accept you.
Please come into my life. I commit it to you."

Acknowledgments

—〰—

I would like to express my gratitude to Jill Foley Turner for her assistance in shaping this manuscript. She worked patiently through many iterations of this book, and I am thankful for her diligent work. I would also like to thank my copyeditor, Jenny Abel, for her excellent work in sharpening and clarifying the manuscript.

Notes

Chapter 1: Your Broken Story

[1]C. S. Lewis, *Mere Christianity* (New York: HarperCollins, 1952), 136-37.

[2]*Dead Poets Society*, directed by Peter Weir (Burbank, CA: Touchstone Pictures, 1989), DVD.

[3]Thomas R. Kelly, *A Testament of Devotion* (New York: Harper and Brothers Press, 1961), chapter 1, "The Light Within."

Chapter 3: The Reversible Paradigm

[1]E. G. Boring, "A New Ambiguous Figure," *The American Journal of Psychology* 42 (1930): 444; and Joseph Jastrow, "Rabbit-Duck Figure," *Popular Science Monthly* (1892): 312.

[2]J. F. Kihlstrom, "Letter to the Editor," *Trends in Cognitive Sciences* 8, issue 11 (November 2004).

[3]P. Brugger and S. Brugger, "The Easter Bunny in October: Is It Disguised as a Duck?," *Perceptual Motor Skills* 76 (1993): 577-78.

Chapter 4: Defining Life Backwards

[1]C. S. Lewis, *The Weight of Glory* (New York: HarperCollins, 2001), 45-46.

[2]C. S. Lewis, *God in the Dock* (Grand Rapids: Eerdmans, 1994), 101.

[3]William R. Moody, *The Life of D. L. Moody* (New York: Fleming H. Revell Company, 1900), 3.

[4]Ibid., 552.

[5]Kurt Vonnegut Jr., *Breakfast of Champions* (New York: Delacorte Press, 1973), 290-95.

[6]C. S. Lewis, *The Last Battle* (New York: Collier Books, 1956), 183-84.

[7]A. W. Tozer, *Who Put Jesus on the Cross?* (Camp Hill, PA: Christian Publications, Inc., 1996), 105.

[8]Wayne A. Grudem, *Bible Doctrine* (Grand Rapids: Zondervan, 1999), 469.

[9]Ibid., 470.

[10]Ibid.

CHAPTER 5: TRUSTING ETERNITY OR CURSING TIME

[1]William Shakespeare, *Troilus and Cressida*, ed. William J. Rolfe (New York: Harper & Brothers, 1905), 111.

[2]H. P. Liddon, *The Divinity of Our Lord and Saviour Jesus Christ* (London: Rivingtons, 1869), 148.

[3]Huston Smith, "Aldous Huxley—A Tribute," *Psychedelic Review* 1, no. 3 (1964): 264-65.

[4]Lee Archie and John G. Archie, "'Art as Unrepressed Wish-Fulfillment' by Sigmund Freud," in *Readings in the History of Aesthetics: An Open-Source Reader; Ver. 0.11* (2006), 425, http://philosophy.lander.edu/intro /artbook.pdf.

[5]Armand Nicholi Jr., *The Question of God* (New York: Free Press, 2002).

[6]Paul Johnson, *Intellectuals* (New York: Harper and Row, 1988).

[7]Bernard Williams, "The Makropulos Case: Reflections on the Tedium of Immorality," in *Problems of the Self* (Cambridge, UK: Cambridge University Press, 1973), 82-106.

[8]Eugene Peterson, *A Long Obedience in the Same Direction* (Downers Grove, IL: InterVarsity Press, 1980). The phrase originally comes from a quote from Friedrich Nietzsche but was redeemed by Peterson in this book on the subject of perseverance.

[9]A. W. Tozer, *Knowledge of the Holy* (New York: HarperCollins, 1961), 52-53.

[10]C. S. Lewis, *Mere Christianity* (New York: HarperCollins, 1952), 136-37.

[11]Tozer, *Knowledge of the Holy*, 52-53.

[12]William Shakespeare, *The Tempest*, ed. Peter Holland (New York: Penguin Books, 1999), 66.

[13]*Waking Ned Devine*, directed by Peter Kirk Jones (Los Angeles: Fox Searchlight Pictures, 1998), DVD.

[14]Lewis, *Mere Christianity*, 136-37.

CHAPTER 6: POETS, SAINTS AND HEROES

[1]*The Two Towers*, directed by Peter Jackson (Los Angeles: New Line Cinema, 2002), DVD.

[2]Adapted from a sermon by Bob Roland of Fellowship Bible Church in Roswell, Georgia.

[3]Thornton Wilder, *Our Town* (New York: Coward-McCann, 1938), 83.

[4]Søren Kierkegaard, *Concluding Unscientific Postscript*, ed. Alastair Hannay (Cambridge, UK: Cambridge University Press, 2009), 307.

[5]Søren Kierkegaard, "An Eternity in Which to Repent," in *Attack Upon "Christendom"* (Princeton, NJ: Princeton University Press, 1968), 246-47.

[6]Ibid.

[7]*The Two Towers*, Jackson.

CHAPTER 7: INSIDE OUT, UPSIDE DOWN AND TALKING TO OURSELVES

[1]*The Two Towers*, directed by Peter Jackson (Los Angeles: New Line Cinema, 2002), DVD.

[2]C. S. Lewis, *Mere Christianity* (New York: Macmillan, 1943), 123.

[3]Cornelius Plantinga Jr., *Not the Way It's Supposed to Be* (Grand Rapids: Eerdmans, 1995), 18.

[4]The Barna Group, "Morality Continues to Decay," November 3, 2003. The survey included core beliefs about homosexuality, sexual fidelity, personal integrity and abortion.

[5]Gary Langer, "Most Americans Say They're Christian," ABC News/ Beliefnet, June 20-24, 2015.

[6]Dallas Willard, *The Divine Conspiracy* (San Francisco: HarperCollins, 1998), chapter 2.

[7]Lewis, *Mere Christianity*, 124.

[8]The Barna Group, "A Biblical Worldview Has a Radical Effect on a Person's Life," December 3, 2003.

[9]Ibid. The study states: "For the purposes of the research, a biblical worldview was defined as believing that absolute moral truths exist; that such truth is defined by the Bible; and firm belief in six specific religious views. Those views were that Jesus Christ lived a sinless life; God is the all-powerful and all-knowing Creator of the universe and He still rules it today; salvation is a gift from God and cannot be earned; Satan is real; a Christian has a responsibility to share their faith in Christ with other people; and the Bible is accurate in all of its teachings. . . . Among the most prevalent alternative worldviews was postmodernism, which seemed to be the dominant perspective among the two youngest generations."

[10]Ibid.

[11]Lewis, *Mere Christianity*, 124.

Chapter 8: Flight Plans, False Goals and a Life Uncommon

[1]Terri Gibbs, "Somebody's Knockin," *Somebody's Knockin'*, MCA Records, 1980.

[2]Erwin W. Lutzer, *Why Good People Do Bad Things* (Nashville, TN: Word Publishing, 2001), 32.

[3]Ibid., 27.

[4]Pieter Brueghel, the Elder, *The Tower of Babel* (one and two), 1563. Oil on boards. Kunsthistorisches Museum, Vienna, and Museum Boijmans Van Beuningen, Rotterdam.

[5]Anne-Geri Gray, "To Dare God," *Christian Woman*, July/August 2000, 24-25.

[6]Ibid.

[7]Charles Dickens, "A Christmas Carol," in *Christmas Books* (Geneva: Oxford University Press, 1941).

[8]James Patterson and Peter Kim, *The Day America Told the Truth* (New York: Plume, 1992), 65-66.

[9]C. S. Lewis, *The Screwtape Letters* (New York: HarperCollins, 1941), 155.

[10]Zach Johnson, E! Online, "Chris Hemsworth Reflects on His Success: 'It Didn't Actually Bring Me the Happiness I Thought It Was Going To'" (originally published in *GQ Australia*, February 2015).

[11]Evangeline Paterson, "Reflection," in *Sightseers into Pilgrims*, ed. Luci Shaw (Wheaton, IL: Tyndale House Publishers, 1973). Used with permission.

Chapter 9: Out of the Woods and Into the Light

[1]Dante Alighieri, *The Divine Comedy*, trans. C. H. Sisson, *Inferno* Canto 1, lines 1-3 (Oxford: Oxford University Press, 1998).

[2]Michael E. Wittmer, *Heaven Is a Place on Earth* (Grand Rapids: Zondervan, 2004), 62.

[3]Ibid.

[4]Alighieri, *Divine Comedy*, *Inferno* Canto 1, lines 31-36, 43.

[5]Alighieri, *Divine Comedy*, *Inferno* Canto 1, lines 44-48.

[6]Os Guinness, *Steering Through Chaos* (Colorado Springs, CO: NavPress, 2000), 35.

[7]C. S. Lewis, *Mere Christianity* (New York: Macmillan, 1942), 111.

[8]Alighieri, *Divine Comedy*, *Inferno* Canto 1, lines 51-63.

[9]Henry Fairlie, *The Seven Deadly Sins Today* (Notre Dame, IN: University of Norte Dame Press, 1979), 175.

Chapter 10: What Do You Seek? (Your Heart's Intention)

[1]A. W. Tozer, *The Knowledge of the Holy* (San Francisco: Harper Collins, 1961), 1.

[2]Charles Dickens, *A Tale of Two Cities* (Mineola, NY: Dover Publications, 1999) 1.

[3]Tozer, *Knowledge of the Holy*, 1.

[4]Phil Organ, "Who Do You Say I Am?," *Anything Through Christ*, Glorify Him Music Ministries, Kingland Records, 1991. Used with permission.

[5]Louie Giglio, *I Am Not, but I Know I Am* (Sisters, OR: Multnomah, 2005), 12-13.

Chapter 11: Becoming a Permanent Marker

[1]Henry Twells, "Time's Paces," in *Hymns and Other Stray Verses* (London: Wells Gardner & Co., 1901), 34.

[2]*City Slickers*, directed by Ron Underwood (Burbank, CA: Castle Rock Entertainment, 1991), DVD.

[3]Paul Bowles, *The Sheltering Sky* (New York: HarperCollins, 1949), 22.

[4]Mont W. Smith, *What the Bible Says About Covenant* (Joplin, MO: College Press, 1996), 48.

[5]William Geist, "Woody Allen: The Rolling Stone Interview," *Rolling Stone*, April 9, 1987.

[6]Woody Allen, *Without Feathers* (New York: Random House, 1975), 99.

[7]Bob Dylan, "Serve Somebody," *Slow Train Coming*, Sony Records, 1979.

Chapter 12: From Theology to Doxology

[1]Vance Havner, *Blood, Bread and Fire: The Christian's Three-Fold Experience* (Grand Rapids: Zondervan, 1939), 47.

[2]The Barna Group, "Barna Survey Examines Changes in Worldview Among Christians Over the Past 13 Years," March 9, 2009.

[3]Ronald J. Sider, *The Scandal of the Evangelical Conscience* (Grand Rapids: Baker Books, 2005), 12-13.

[4]Havner, *Blood, Bread and Fire*, 47.

[5]Ibid., 48.

[6]The Holocaust: Crimes, Heroes and Villains, "The Village," www.auschwitz .dk/Trocme.htm.

[7]Ibid.

[8]Ibid.

[9]Havner, *Blood, Bread and Fire*, 48.

[10]Tim Hansel, *When I Relax I Feel Guilty* (Elgin, IL: David C. Cook Publishing Co., 1979), 53.

EPILOGUE

[1]Charles W. Colson, *Born Again* (Grand Rapids: Chosen Books, 2008), 103.

[2]Ibid., 102.

[3]Ibid., 104, 122.

[4]Ibid., 112.

[5]Ibid., 124.

[6]C. S. Lewis, *Mere Christianity* (New York: Macmillan, 1960), 111.

[7]Colson, *Born Again*, 125.

[8]Lewis, *Mere Christianity*, 112.

[9]Colson, *Born Again*, 141.

[10]Ibid., 129.

[11]Ibid.

[12]Ibid.

[13]Ibid., 133.

[14]Ibid., 147.

[15]Ibid., 148.

[16]Jonathan Aitken, *Charles W. Colson: A Life Redeemed* (New York: Waterbook Press, 2005), 218.

[17]Al Quie, "Charles W. Colson Memorial Service at National Cathedral," Washington National Cathedral, Washington, DC, May 21, 2012, http://chuckcolson.org/memorial-service.

[18]Aitken, *A Life Redeemed*, 219.

[19]Colson, *Born Again*, 172.

[20]*Impeachment: Selected Materials, Committee on the Judiciary, House of Representatives, One Hundred Fifth Congress*, chairman Henry J. Hyde (Washington, DC: Government Printing Office, 1998), 181.

[21]Colson, *Born Again*, 255-56.

[22]Aitken, *A Life Redeemed*, 259.

[23]UPI, "Colson's Son Seized in Raid," *The Milwaukee Journal*, January 25, 1975.

[24]Colson, *Born Again*, 421.

[25]Aitken, *A Life Redeemed*, 268.

[26]Ibid., 269.

[27]Ibid., 271.

[28]Eric Metaxas, *Seven Men and the Secret of Their Greatness* (Nashville, TN: Thomas Nelson, 2013), 185.

[29]Aitken, *A Life Redeemed*, 274.

[30]Emily Colson, "Charles W. Colson Memorial Service at National Cathedral," Washington National Cathedral, Washington, DC, May 21, 2012, http://chuckcolson.org/memorial-service.

[31]Ibid.

[32]Danny Croce, "Charles W. Colson Memorial Service at National Cathedral," Washington National Cathedral, Washington, DC, May 21, 2012, http://chuckcolson.org/memorial-service.

[33]Mitch McConnell, http://chuckcolson.org/tributes.

About the Author

Dr. Kenneth Boa is engaged in a ministry of relational evangelism and discipleship, teaching, writing and speaking. He holds a BS from Case Institute of Technology, a ThM from Dallas Theological Seminary, a PhD from New York University and a DPhil from the University of Oxford in England.

Ken is engaged in a wide variety of ministry activities. On a local level, he teaches four studies a week and leads seven small discipleship groups on a monthly basis. He is also engaged in one-on-one discipleship, mentoring and spiritual direction. Ken's Reflections Ministries also involves people in special outreach events and conferences. On a national and international level, Ken does an extensive amount of speaking and teaching throughout the United States and in various countries. He also creates numerous written, audio, visual and video resources, and continues to expand the kenboa .org website as a resource center for people around the world.